D0705608

Learning to use statistical tests in psychology

THIRD EDITION

Learning to use statistical tests in psychology

THIRD EDITION

**Judith Greene
and
Manuela D'Oliveira**

Open University Press

Open University Press
McGraw-Hill Education
McGraw-Hill House
Shoppenhangers Road
Maidenhead
Berkshire
England
SL6 2QL

email: enquiries@openup.co.uk
world wide web: www.openup.co.uk

and Two Penn Plaza, New York, NY 10121-2289, USA

First published 1982
Reprinted 1983, 1985, 1987, 1988, 1989, 1990, 1992, 1993, 1994, 1995, 1996, 1998

First published in second edition, 1999
Reprinted 2000, 2001

First published in this third edition, 2006

Copyright © Judith Greene and Manuela D'Oliveira, 2006

All rights reserved. Except for the quotation of short passages for the purpose
of criticism and review, no part of this publication may be reproduced, stored
in a retrieval system, or transmitted, in any form or by any means, electronic,
mechanical, photocopying, recording or otherwise, without the prior written
permission of the publisher or a licence from the Copyright Licensing Agency
Limited. Details of such licences (for reprographic reproduction) may be
obtained from the Copyright Licensing Agency Ltd of 90 Tottenham Court
Road, London, W1T 4LP.

A catalogue record of this book is available from the British Library

ISBN-13: 978 0335 21680 3 (pb)   978 0335 21681 1 (hb)
ISBN-10: 0335 21680 3(pb)   0335 21681 1 (hb)

Library of Congress Cataloging-in-Publication Data
CIP data has been applied for

Typeset by RefineCatch Limited, Bungay, Suffolk
Printed in the UK by Bell & Bain Ltd, Glasgow

To Norman, Kate and Matthew

and

To Pedro, Maria João, Catarina, Miguel, Mariana, Carolina

Contents

Preface to the third edition

There have been an enormous number of textbooks claiming to present statistics in a simple way. Despite this, many psychology students still find the whole statistical business something of a mystery. How does this book differ from these other attempts?

We believe that virtually all books on statistics feel obliged to start with the mathematical principles underlying probability distributions, samples and populations, and statistical testing. But, however simply these are presented, in our view they obscure the basic reasons why psychologists use statistical tests.

So we had better come clean straight away. This book sets out to achieve one aim. This is to enable students to select appropriate statistical tests to evaluate the significance of data obtained from psychological research. In other words, this book is concerned with *inferential statistics* as used in psychological studies.

We have concentrated on this to the exclusion of much else. Topics such as descriptive statistics and the basic principles of probability are well covered in other statistical texts. There is nothing here about the use of surveys, observational techniques or psychometric tests of intelligence and personality. All we have included is the battery of statistical tests which are usually introduced to psychology students as part of their undergraduate laboratory course. We hope that, by aiming at a single target, we will maximize our chances of scoring a bull's-eye.

This 'beginners' book takes students from the simplest non-parametric tests, like the Wilcoxon test, through to complex analysis of variance designs. The principle is the same throughout: always to give the rationale for using appropriate statistical analyses for particular research designs. It is certainly our expectation that anyone who has mastered the why and how of the statistical tests given in this book will be in a position to understand the basic principles of statistical tests as presented in advanced textbooks of psychological statistics.

Our belief is that, with the aid of this book, students will feel comfortable about the basis for selecting and applying all kinds of statistical tests. We hope that teachers will wish to use a book which frees students from much of the panic usually associated with statistics. That way they should be in a far more receptive state to learn.

One major change in this third edition is that the book is now organized into four parts. Part I consists of a general introduction to the principles of psychological research and psychological statistics. Part II describes statistical tests for straightforward experiments with two and three conditions. Part III introduces the statistical tests based on ANOVA designs. It also considers tests for multiple comparisons between individual conditions.

Part IV is a new part. By omitting some of the less used non-parametric tests, we have been able to bring together the statistical tests suitable for analysing relationships between variables, including correlation and regression.

Another innovation is to devote a whole chapter to each statistical test, making it easier to draw attention to the special requirements for each test. These additions will make the book more comprehensive in line with the range of tests generally available.

Study guide for students

The aim of this book is to explain the rationale for using statistical tests to evaluate the results of psychological research. The problem is that in psychology you have to carry out these experiments on *human beings*, often other students. Unlike most physical objects, human beings are unique, each interpreting and performing whatever task you set them in a slightly different way.

You will find that the data and observations obtained from the people doing a psychological experiment are often extremely varied and that many of the things which influence their behaviour may have nothing to do with the aims of the research. It is for this reason that you have to sort out whether experimental results are really significant. And, as you will see, this is just what statistical tests enable you to do.

You will probably be relieved to hear that the chapters which introduce the basic rationale for statistics and summarize all you need to know in order to select an appropriate statistical test are the shortest chapters in the book. These are aspects of using statistical tests that students often find rather puzzling, but we hope that these chapters will clear up all your worries.

Other chapters in the book present statistical tests, explaining the rationale for each one, taking you 'step by step' through any necessary calculations and giving precise instructions about how to use the statistical tables at the back of the book. For more complex types of statistical analysis you will be introduced to the latest types of computer programs for carrying out numerical calculations.

One essential feature of this book is the *questions* which occur throughout the text. It is not enough to read the summaries presented in the *progress boxes*. The only way you can make sure that you understand the context of each section is to attempt the questions *before* looking up the answers at the back! It is equally important to work your way through the step-by-step instructions given for each statistical test. Otherwise, you will never gain the confidence which comes from fully understanding the rationale for a statistical test.

Let us end by making some important and, we hope, encouraging points. The first thing to grasp is that statistical tests are not magic formulae to be turned to, desperately wondering which on earth to choose. They simply follow as a natural result of the kind of research you have chosen to do. What makes most people give up all hope of mastering statistics is the thought that they will find themselves presented with a huge amount of numerical data without the foggiest idea of how to deal with them. But this is quite the wrong way to go about things. The important thing is to decide what research you want to carry out. You will find that such a decision immediately narrows your possible choice of statistical tests to only one or two, and that there are good reasons for selecting one or the other.

With statistical tests selection is all; the actual calculations are quite easy once you have understood the reasons for doing them. The aim has been to introduce the principles of using statistical tests *without referring to any mathematical concepts*. And, in order to do the calculations for the tests themselves, you will only need to know how to add, subtract, multiply, divide and square numbers. With modern pocket calculators and computer programs this really should be child's play.

Good luck – and if, in spite of everything, you do find yourself getting disheartened by statistics, turn back and reread this study guide.

Acknowledgements

Grateful acknowledgement is made to the following sources for permission to reprint the tables in this book:

Table A from F. Wilcoxon and R.A. Wilcox, *Some Rapid Approximate Statistical Procedures*, American Cyanamid Co., 1949;

Table B from R.P. Runyon and A. Haber, *Fundamentals of Behavioral Statistics*, 3rd edn, Reading, Mass., Addison-Wesley, 1976;

Table C from D.V. Lindley and J.C.P. Miller, *Cambridge Elementary Statistical Tables*, 10th edn, Cambridge University Press, 1973;

Table D from M. Friedman, 'The use of ranks to avoid the assumption of normality implicit in the analysis of variance' in *Journal of the American Statistical Association*, Vol. 32, 1937;

Table E from D.V. Lindley and J.C.P. Miller, *Cambridge Elementary Statistical Tables*, 10th edn, Cambridge University Press, 1973;

Table F from W.H. Kruskal and W.A. Wallis, 'Use of ranks in one-criterion variance analysis' in *Journal of the American Statistical Association*, Vol. 47, 1952;

Table G from D.V. Lindley and J.C.P. Miller, *Cambridge Elementary Statistical Tables*, 10th edn, Cambridge University Press, 1973;

Table H from Table VII (p. 63) of R.A. Fisher and F. Yates, *Statistical Tables for Biological, Agricultural and Medical Research* (6th edition), published by Longman Group Ltd, London, 1974 (previously published by Oliver & Boyd Ltd, Edinburgh).

Part I   Introduction

1   Research in psychology

1.1   Psychological research and statistics

You may be wondering why a book on learning to use statistical tests in psychology would start with an introduction to the general principles of psychological research. You may be pleased to hear that psychologists do not study statistics for its own sake. Statistical tests simply provide a tool for analysing the results of psychological research.

The aim of psychological research is to test psychological theories about human behaviour. Researchers make predictions about human behaviour in order to test whether the results of the research support the prediction or not.

Once you appreciate that the point of psychological research is to test research predictions, you will find that learning to select and use statistical tests will be reasonably straightforward.

1.2   Variability in human behaviour

One of the particular aspects of humans is that they vary a great deal in their characteristics and behaviour. So it is difficult for psychologists to make predictions that will apply to all human beings in exactly the same way. Even identical twins develop differently, depending on circumstances.

For this reason, psychological researchers make predictions in a way that reflects the variability in human behaviour.

The variability between humans is formulated as variables. The aim of psychological research is to study variables in human behaviour.

1.3   Relationships between variables

The major implication for psychological research is that predictions are made about relationships between variables in human behaviour.

Let us take an example of measuring children's scores for reading and arithmetic. One thing is certain. All the children will not have exactly the same reading scores. Proficiency in reading will be very variable. For this reason, reading scores represent a variable.

The same would apply to the children's arithmetic scores. Again the arithmetic scores are likely to vary from child to child over quite a wide range. For this reason, arithmetic scores represent a variable.

The researcher would be interested in testing whether the children who have high scores on reading also have high scores on arithmetic. The aim would be to discover whether there is a relationship between these two variables. One of the two variables is the variable of reading scores and the second variable is the variable of arithmetic scores.

1.4   Research hypothesis

In psychological research a prediction about relationships between variables is formulated as a research hypothesis. A research hypothesis might predict that there will be a relationship between reading scores and arithmetic scores. The aim of psychological research is to test whether the research hypothesis is supported by the scores of the children on both variables.

The research hypothesis predicts a relationship between variables. It is called a hypothesis because it is something that is proposed and has to be tested.

1.5   Null hypothesis

One especially important point is that, in order to test a research hypothesis, it must be possible for the predicted relationships between variables to be supported or not to be supported. If it were always certain that the prediction would be supported there would be no point in doing psychological research.

In our example, the predicted relationship between the variables of reading scores and arithmetic scores may or may not be supported by the children's scores on these two variables. It may turn out that the children's scores do not support the predicted relationship between reading and arithmetic.

This is a basic rule of psychological research. A research hypothesis is always tested against a null hypothesis, which states that a researcher will not find the research results he/she expects. According to the null hypothesis, any results found in a research study are due to random variability in the children's scores rather than the prediction that the researcher is interested in testing.

1.6 Rationale for using statistical tests

The next question is how to set about showing whether there is indeed a predicted relationship between the variables of children's reading scores and arithmetic scores. The issue is whether it is possible to rule out the null hypothesis.

Because human behaviour is variable, it is not easy to rule out the possibility that the reading and arithmetic scores are random scores. Perhaps the scores of the children taking part in the research are so variable that the null hypothesis of random variability in scores cannot be rejected.

The rationale for using statistical tests is to measure how much variability there is in children's scores. Do the scores support the research hypothesis that reading scores and arithmetic scores are related? Or is there just too much random variability in the scores?

Psychologists use statistical tests to decide between these two outcomes. Do the scores support the research hypothesis or are the scores random, as stated by the null hypothesis?

1.7 Participants in psychological research

This is a good point at which to introduce a modern terminology to describe the people taking part in psychological research. These people are called *participants*. This term is used to indicate that the people are actively participating in psychological research.

An older term used for the people taking part in psychological research (especially in experiments) was 'subjects'. This was originally used in order to differentiate human subjects from the objects used in scientific research. Although the term 'subjects' has now been replaced by 'participants', you will still come across subjects in older articles in psychological journals and in some textbooks on statistics. We will be using the term 'participants' and will only refer to subjects as an alternative term when the term subject is always used.

Progress box one

- Psychologists study human beings, who are variable in their behaviour.
- Psychologists make predictions about relationships between variables, formulated as a research hypothesis.
- This is contrasted with a null hypothesis, which states the possibility that the predicted relationships will not occur because of random variability in scores.
- Statistical tests are used to decide between the research hypothesis and the null hypothesis.
- The people taking part in psychological research are called participants.

2 Experiments in psychology

2.1 The experimental method

In experimental research, as in all psychological research, experimenters make predictions about relationships between variables when predicting human behaviour. They have to take into account the variability in humans so that their predictions are probabilities about how participants will react rather than certainties.

The special feature of experiments is that an experimenter selects one of the variables to test whether this variable has any effect on a second variable.

An example would be an experimenter giving children a reading scheme and measuring the effects of the reading scheme on the children's scores on a reading test. These are both variables. One variable varies between giving a reading scheme and not giving a reading scheme. The children's scores are a variable because the scores will vary from child to child.

The research hypothesis predicts the effects of the reading scheme variable on the variable of children's scores. The research hypothesis has to be compared with the null hypothesis that there are random differences in the children's scores.

2.2 Independent and dependent variables

We will now introduce the terminology of independent variables and dependent variables in experimental research. The variable that the researcher decides to test is known as the *independent variable*. This is because the 'reading scheme' and 'no reading scheme' conditions are selected independently by the experimenter before the experiment even begins.

The second variable, representing children's scores, is known as the *dependent variable*. This is because the reading scores are dependent on the way in which the experimenter first selects the independent variable of the reading scheme.

In order to test the prediction in the research hypothesis the experimenter decides to vary an independent variable to see whether this has any effect on the dependent variable. In the reading scheme experiment the researcher selects one variable (reading scheme or no reading scheme) to see what effect this will have on the second variable (children's reading scores). The aim is to test the predicted independent variable and to attempt to rule out other irrelevant variables that might also be affecting participants' behaviour. The remainder of this chapter will discuss various ways in which experimenters attempt to eliminate the effects of irrelevant variables.

2.3   Experimental and control conditions

The basic experimental design is for the researcher to allocate participants to experimental conditions representing the independent variable. A comparison is made between participants' scores on the dependent variable. For instance, children would be allocated to the reading scheme condition or the no reading scheme condition and their reading scores would be measured.

The problem is that all the children might show an improvement in reading scores over time, regardless of whether they had been given a reading scheme or not. Can the experimenter be certain that any improvement in reading is due to the reading scheme?

Experimenters always try to rule out irrelevant variables that are not predicted by the research hypothesis. In order to achieve this, experimenters try to design an experiment in which the only difference between the two conditions is due to the predicted effects of the independent variable formulated in the research hypothesis.

It is for this reason that experimenters often introduce a control condition against which the effects of an independent variable can be compared. The point about a control condition is that it represents a condition in which people are not subjected to the experimental condition. So it is possible to compare two conditions, one with the reading scheme and one without the reading scheme. The experimental design would be:

Experimental condition
Reading scheme   Reading scores

Control condition
No reading scheme   Reading scores

The prediction would be that there is more improvement in the reading scores for the experimental condition than for the control condition. The researcher might find some general improvement in scores for both conditions due to other variables such as a new teacher. However, if there is a more improvement in the experimental condition, it can be claimed that this extra improvement is due not to factors that might have affected both conditions equally but to the reading scheme which affected only the experimental condition and not the control condition.

Sometimes, rather than comparing an experimental and a control condition, it is more appropriate to compare two levels of an independent variable. An example would be an experiment to investigate whether lists of common words are easier to remember than lists of rare words. The experimental design would compare recall scores under two experimental conditions:

Experimental condition 1
Learning lists of common words   Recall of words

Experimental condition 2
Learning lists of rare words   Recall of words

? Question 2.1 Suppose a researcher is testing a research hypothesis that common words are more easily recalled than rare words.

(a) What is the independent variable?

(b) What is the dependent variable?

(c) Would higher recall scores in experimental condition 1 support the research hypothesis?

2.4 Three or more experimental conditions

So far we have been talking about comparing only two experimental conditions. But researchers might want to look at more than two conditions to test an independent variable. For instance, they might be interested in investigating whether learning a list of vary rare words, a list of fairly common words and a list of very common words would have an effect on participants' ability to recall the lists of words:

Experimental condition 1
Learning lists of very rare words

Experimental condition 2
Learning lists of fairly common words

Experimental condition 3
Learning lists of very common words

You would still be testing one independent variable but with three experimental conditions. The research hypothesis would be that participants would have better recall scores for the list of very common words.

2.5   Same participants (related designs)

The next important decision to be made is whether to use the same participants for all conditions or whether to use groups of different participants in each condition. As we shall see, both these options have advantages and disadvantages.

From the point of view of reducing individual differences between participants, there is a case for using the same participants for all conditions. The rationale is that, when using the same participants, everything about the participants will be the same in all conditions. If one individual participant is highly motivated when learning one list of words, he/she will also be highly motivated when learning other lists of words.

Using the same participants is known as a *related* design. Because the comparison is with the same participants, the scores from each participant are related.

The main disadvantage of using the same participants for all conditions is that all participants are exposed to all the experimental conditions. The experimenter has to take into account the possibility that participants may be affected by their experience of earlier conditions.

In the attempt to reduce these order effects, it is normal practice for researchers to vary the order of conditions so that half the subjects learn list A first and list B second and the other half learn list B first and list A second. The idea is that any irrelevant effects of learning from experience are likely to be equalized by reversing the order of the conditions. This is known as *counterbalancing* the order of conditions.

2.6   Different participants (unrelated designs)

Another option is to use groups of different participants for each experimental condition. There are some cases when it is obvious that different participants are required. Imagine that you are interested in whether boys or girls are more likely to benefit from a reading scheme. There is simply no way in which the same children could be allocated to the boys or girls group. There would have to be different groups of girls and boys.

The main advantage of using different participants for each condition is that each participant is only exposed to one condition. Because of this there can be no order effects of one condition on another condition. Using different participants is always the best option if it is considered that exposure to one condition may have an effect on another condition.

Using different participants is known as an *unrelated* design. Because the comparison is between participants the scores from each participant are unrelated.

The problem is how to allocate different participants to each of the experimental conditions. Perhaps all the participants who are the best learners might be allocated to one condition. Alternatively, all the participants who cannot be bothered may be allocated to another group.

One method is to try to match the participants. The experimenter might give participants a prior memory test in order to identify the best learners. The experimenter could then allocate equal numbers of good learners and not-so-good learners to each group.

Another method is to allocate participants at random to each of the conditions. If participants are randomly allocated to experimental conditions, then people of different ages or abilities are just as likely to be found in all the experimental groups.

All this goes to show how many things have to be taken into account when designing an experiment. The point is to try to eliminate all possible irrelevant variables that might be affecting participants. The only differences between the two conditions should be the predicted differences due to the independent variable.

 Progress box two

- Experimenters decide on an independent variable and predict the effect of this variable on the dependent variable of participants' scores.
- Experimenters select experimental conditions to test the research hypothesis.
- Experimenters attempt to rule out irrelevant variables that are not predicted by the research hypothesis.
- An advantage of related designs is fewer individual differences between the same participants doing all experimental conditions. Experimenters need to counterbalance possible order effects.
- Unrelated designs are suitable when it is important that different participants should only do one experimental condition. Individual differences between participants can be offset by matching participants or by randomly allocating participants to different conditions.

3 Selecting statistical tests

3.1 Basic principles for selecting tests

Now we come to the all-important chapter as far as your ability to select statistical tests is concerned. You should be encouraged to note that this is one of the shortest chapters in the book. The vital consideration is to choose an appropriate statistical test for each type of research. The whole art of using statistics is to match up research designs with the statistical tests listed in the remaining chapters of this book

We have constantly emphasized that there is a lot of variability in participants' scores caused by individual differences. This means that every research hypothesis has to be compared against a null hypothesis that there is random variability in scores. Each statistical test will be appropriate for designs that produce different amounts of random variability.

So the first and most important point we want to emphasize is this: the selection of an appropriate statistical test follows from the design you have chosen to test your research hypothesis. Choice of a suitable test depends on a few decisions about research designs. Once you have made these decisions you will find that you have automatically selected the appropriate statistical test to use for analysing your research data.

3.2 Experiments

Many of the statistical tests described in this book are designed to test the results of experiments. Experiments test predictions about differences between conditions as a result of the experimenter deciding to test an independent variable.

In later chapters you will be introduced to other statistical tests, which are suitable for testing other types of relationships between variables.

3.3 Number of experimental conditions

An important aspect of a research design is how many experimental conditions there are in an experiment.

Some statistical tests are designed to analyse experiments with only two conditions.

Experimental designs with three or more conditions require more complex statistical comparisons between conditions.

3.4 Related or unrelated designs

One of the most important criteria for selecting a statistical test depends on whether the same participants have been used for all conditions (related design) or whether groups of different participants have been used for each condition (unrelated design).

3.5 Non-parametric or parametric tests

There are two main kids of statistical tests described in this book, called *non-parametric* tests and *parametric* tests. The way these tests are identified depends on how the scores (known as data) are measured.

Non-parametric tests are based on ordinal data. 'Ordinal data' refers to scores that can be ranked in order from lowest score to highest score.

Parametric tests are based on interval data. 'Interval data' refers to scores in which the intervals between scores are equal, making it possible to carry out numerical calculations.

You do not need to worry about this brief introduction to these different types of tests. Details will be given for every type of statistical test described in this book.

3.6 Using the Decision Chart

The Decision Chart (inside back cover) consists of a set of questions you will have to answer in order to identify an appropriate statistical test.

Questions will be asked for each statistical test, and answers suggested. In every case, if you answer these questions in the Decision Chart, you will inevitably discover the correct statistical test.

Progress box three

- There are a few easy decisions to be made in order to select a statistical test.
- All the appropriate statistical tests are contained in the Decision Chart.
- For each type of test, appropriate questions are asked in the Decision Chart.

4 Using statistical tests

4.1 Variability in data

However much experimenters try to eliminate irrelevant variables in their experimental designs, they can never get rid of all the variability in participants' scores. This variability in scores will inevitably be reflected in whatever measure you take of the dependent variable. What you want to know is this: are the differences in the scores the result of manipulating the independent variable? Or is there only random variability in the scores, as stated by the null hypothesis?

Suppose the research hypothesis is that participants will have better memory recall for simple texts than for complex texts. The independent variable consists of giving one group of participants a simple text to read and another group a complex text. The number of ideas recalled is the measure of the dependent variable.

After running the experiment you may end up with recall scores for each condition, as shown in Table 4.1. Total scores are given for each condition. The means represent average scores calculated by dividing the totals by the number of participants, in this case 10 participants in each condition. It is clear that the data in Table 4.1 show that mean scores for number of ideas recalled is higher in Condition 1 than in Condition 2.

? Question 4.1   Does the difference between the means support the research hypothesis?

There would be no problem about claiming support for the hypothesis if each and every participant in Condition 1 had recalled exactly 6.4 ideas while every participant in Condition 2 had recalled 3.6 ideas. In that case it

Table 4.1   Number of ideas recalled

	Condition 1 (simple texts)	Condition 2 (complex texts)
	10	2
	5	1
	6	3
	3	4
	9	4
	8	4
	7	2
	5	5
	6	7
	5	4
Totals	64	36
Means	6.4	3.6

would be obvious that the participants in Condition 1 recalled more ideas than in Condition 2.

But life is not that easy. There may be a lot of variability in scores that has nothing to do with the predicted differences between simple and complex texts.

If you look at the scores in Table 4.1 you will notice that participants' scores varied in the two conditions. For instance, although the scores were generally higher in Condition 1, there was one participant in Condition 1 who recalled only 3 ideas in the simple text. Many participants scored more ideas in the complex text.

? Question 4.2   (a) In Table 4.1 how many participants in both conditions recalled 5 ideas?

(b) What were the lowest and highest scores in Condition 1?

(c) What were the lowest and highest scores in Condition 2?

It is obvious from the scores in Table 4.1 that there is quite a lot of variability in the number of correct ideas recalled. Clearly, means do not tell us everything we need to know about participants' scores. We also need a measure of the total variability of scores.

We now get to the heart of the rationale for statistical tests, which is to measure the amount of variability in the data. Does the difference between the means indicate significant support for the research hypothesis?

Alternatively, are the differences between conditions swamped by the total variability in scores, as stated by the null hypothesis?

4.2   Probabilities in statistical tables

A big difference in mean scores between conditions may be due to the predicted effects of the independent variable rather than random variability. But there is always a specific probability that the differences in scores are caused by random variability. So there can never be 100 per cent certainty that the scores in an experiment are due to the effects of selecting the independent variable.

Statistical tests calculate probabilities that results are significant. The way this is done may seem rather paradoxical. Statistical tables provide probabilities that any differences in scores are due to random variability, as stated by the null hypothesis. This means that the less probable it is that any differences are due to random variability, the more justification there is for rejecting the null hypothesis.

This is the basis of all statistical tests. Statistical tables give the probability that scores in an experiment occur on a random basis. If the probability that the scores are random is very low, then you can reject the null hypothesis that the differences are random. Instead you can accept the research hypothesis that the experimental results are significant, that is, that they are not likely to be random.

Strictly speaking, the only conclusion from looking up probabilities in statistical tables is that they justify rejecting the null hypothesis. But you will find that, if the null hypothesis can be rejected, psychological researchers usually claim that the results provide support for the predictions in the research hypothesis.

4.3   Selecting a level of significance

So far we have not really tackled the question of why a researcher would be prepared to accept a particular percentage probability of random variability when deciding whether or not to reject the null hypothesis. What risk would be acceptable that the scores resulting from the experiment occurred randomly, as stated by the null hypothesis, and were not significant at all? Of course, you would like to be 100 per cent certain that the difference in scores is significant. But, as we said earlier, you can never be 100 per cent certain that the total scores are not randomly distributed.

Would you accept a 99 per cent probability that your results are significant against a 1 per cent probability that they are random? Or would you accept a 95 per cent probability of significance against a 5 per cent probability that the scores are random?

These percentage probabilities are known as *levels of significance*. There is no simple answer as to what level of significance is acceptable. It is up to experimenters to decide what odds they are prepared to accept when deciding whether the results of an experiment are significant. For this reason, experimenters always have to state the percentage probability of random variability that they will accept for rejecting the null hypothesis.

Imagine that you are investigating whether a new reading scheme might help children to read. You carried out an experiment in which you compared the progress of a group of children using your new scheme against a control group using traditional methods. Suppose the probability that this difference could have occurred randomly was 5 per cent. This represents a 1 in 20 chance that the scores are random. Would you accept that the difference was significant and introduce the new reading scheme, and at what cost in materials and teacher training?

Imagine another case when you are testing a powerful drug with nasty side-effects and find an improvement in patients taking the drug as compared with a control group. If the difference between the groups could have occurred by chance 5 in 100 times, would you accept that the difference is significant and introduce the new drug? Would you change your odds if you knew that without the drug most of the patients would die anyway? And how would you feel if an aeroplane you were going to fly in had a 5 per cent probability of developing electrical failure?

These examples bring home the fact that choosing a significance level is always a matter of deciding what odds you are prepared to accept that your results are due to random variability. In psychology (possibly because it is thought that nothing too terrible can happen as a result of accepting a result as significant!) there is a convention to accept probabilities of either 1 per cent or 5 per cent as grounds for rejecting the null hypothesis.

The way levels of significance are expressed is to state that the probability of a result being due to random variability is less than 1 per cent or less than 5 per cent. That is why in articles in psychological journals you will see statements that differences between experimental conditions are 'significant ($p < 0.01$)' or 'significant ($p < 0.05$)'. This means that the probability (p) of a result occurring by chance is less than (expressed as $<$) 1 per cent (0.01) or 5 per cent (0.05).

Sometimes, you will find other probabilities quoted, such as $p < 0.02$ or $p < 0.001$. These represent probabilities of obtaining a random result 2 times in 100 and 1 time in 1000 (2 per cent and 0.1 per cent). These percentage probabilities give you grounds for rejecting the null hypothesis that your results are due to the effects of random variability.

? **Question 4.3**   Which of the following percentage probabilities represents the smallest probability of random scores?

1 in 100 ($p < 0.01$), 1 in 20 ($p < 0.05$), 1 in 1000 ($p < 0.001$)

We have so far been discussing cases when the probability of random variability is quite low. But sometimes there may be a probability of random variability that is too high to justify rejecting the null hypothesis. A probability of 10% is considered to be too high a probability of random variability to be able to reject the null hypothesis. In this case, the null hypothesis cannot be rejected so there is no significant support for the research hypothesis.

4.4   One-tailed and two-tailed hypotheses

There is one further point about the way an experimental hypothesis is formulated which has implications for the way in which you look up probabilities in statistical tables. This is whether the research hypothesis is a *one-tailed* or a *two-tailed* hypothesis.

A one-tailed hypothesis is one that, as its name implies, makes a prediction in one particular direction. An example might be that more ideas will be recalled in a simple text than in a complex text.

With a one-tailed hypothesis the results will only be significant if they are in the predicted direction. If a significant difference is found in the opposite direction – that more ideas are recalled from complex texts – this will not count, because it was not predicted.

A two-tailed hypothesis makes a prediction that the effect of an independent variable may go in either direction. The prediction would be that more ideas might be recalled either from a simple text or from a complex text, that is, predicting that simple or complex texts will have some effect on recall but not being prepared to say what.

A two-tailed hypothesis is much vaguer than a one-tailed hypothesis. There are also differences in assessing the probabilities for a two-tailed hypothesis.

You will find in statistical tables that there are different probabilities for one-tailed and two-tailed hypotheses. Because a two-tailed hypothesis makes two predictions, one in each direction, the levels of significance have to be stricter. A one-tailed hypothesis has a specific percentage probability, but for a two-tailed hypothesis there is double the probability in either direction.

Do not worry about this distinction between one-tailed and two-tailed hypotheses at this stage. You will be given detailed instructions about what to do for each statistical test.

 Progress box four

- Experimenters predict differences in scores between conditions.
- There will always be random variability in scores that is not due to the predicted differences.
- Statistical tables provide probabilities of random variability, as stated by the null hypothesis.
- If the probability of random variability is low the null hypothesis can be rejected.
- Experimenters select a level of significance, usually $p < 0.05$ or $p < 0.01$.
- If the data attain these levels of significance the null hypothesis is rejected and instead the data are claimed as supporting the research hypothesis.
- A one-tailed hypothesis predicts results in one direction only. A two-tailed hypothesis predicts results in either direction.

Part II Statistical tests for experiments

5 Introduction to non-parametric tests

5.1 Ordinal data

The statistical tests described in this chapter are non-parametric tests. For each type of statistical test there is a type of measurement that is suitable for that test. In the case of non-parametric statistical tests ordinal data are suitable. The main feature of ordinal data is that the scores can be ranked in order from the lowest score to the highest score.

Non-parametric tests comparing participants' scores in experimental conditions are made on the basis of whether scores can be ranked as higher or lower in different conditions.

Ranking the scores in two experimental conditions from lowest score to highest score is a good way of testing a research hypothesis about whether the scores in one of the experimental conditions are ranked higher than the scores in the other condition.

In the rest of this chapter we will be giving some general tips for ranking scores. The methods of ranking for particular non-parametric tests will be introduced when those tests are described.

5.2 Assigning ranks to scores

In order to establish which scores are higher or lower it is necessary to rank scores in terms of their relative size from lowest to highest. In order to rank scores you have to assign ranks of 1, 2, 3, 4, etc. to each score in order of their magnitude, starting with the smallest score. The most usual way of ranking scores is to give the lowest rank to the lowest score and the highest rank to the highest score. This makes it easier to see which are the lowest scores and which are the highest scores.

You will notice that we have assigned ranks to all the scores in Table 5.1. The first step is to identify the lowest score in Table 5.1, which is 3. We

Table 5.1   Ranking scores

Scores	Ranks
6	4
3	1
12	7
4	2
7	5
5	3
8	6

allocate a rank of 1 to the lowest score of 3. The next lowest score of 4 is allocated a rank of 2. The next lowest score of 5 is ranked as 3. The rest of the ranks are allocated in the same way, ending up with the highest score of 12 being assigned the highest rank of 7. A good tip for calculating number or ranks is to check that there are seven scores in Table 5.1. This means that there should be seven ranks in all.

 Question 5.1   In Table 5.1 what rank has been assigned to the score of 7, and why?

5.3   Assigning tied ranks

We now need to consider any problems that might rise from assigning tied ranks to identical scores. In Table 5.1 each score was different from all the other scores. This made it easy to allocate a single rank to each of the scores.

But in some sets of scores some of the participants may have exactly the same recall scores. For example, one participant may have a score of 4 and another participant also has the same score of 4. These two scores of 4 are identical. How is it possible to assign tied ranks to these two scores?

There are special rules for dealing with cases when there are identical scores. If you look at the scores in Table 5.2, you will see that three participants have recall scores of 1 and two participants have both scored 4.

What ranks should be assigned to the three scores of 1? Should these scores all be given rank 1 because they are the lowest scores?

The basic procedure is to assign the three scores the average of the ranks they would have been entitled to. The three scores of 1 in Table 5.2 would have been assigned ranks 1, 2 and 3 because these are the three lowest scores. All three scores are given the average of these ranks: $1 + 2 + 3 = 6$,

Table 5.2   Assigning tied ranks

Scores	Ranks
1	2
2	4
1	2
4	6.5
1	2
3	5
4	6.5
6	9
5	8

and $6 \div 3 = 2$. This result is that the three scores of 1 are each assigned the average rank of 2.

Because the ranks of 1, 2 and 3 have already been used up for the three lowest scores of 1, the next available rank of 4 is allocated to the next lowest score of 2. The next rank of 5 is allocated to the next lowest score of 3.

But what is to be done about the two identical scores of 4? The two scores of 4 would have been entitled to the next available ranks of 6 and 7. Since the average of 6 and 7 is 6.5 the two scores of 4 are both assigned ranks of 6.5.

The next score of 5 will be assigned the next available rank of 8 and the highest score of 6 gets the highest rank of 9.

Especially when there are complicated tied ranks, it is a useful tip to count the total number of scores (in this case, 9 scores). The aim is to check whether the highest rank of 9 has been correctly assigned to the highest score of 6.

5.4   Standard headings for presenting statistical tests

When we describe the non-parametric statistical tests for two conditions in Chapters 6 and 7, we shall be presenting each test under a standard set of headings. In fact, we will be presenting all the statistical tests in this book under the same set of headings. The aim is to make it simple for you to follow the rationale and detailed instructions required for each statistical test and how to look up the probabilities in statistical tables.

The standard headings for each statistical test are given below:

1 *When to use*. In this section you are reminded of the experimental designs for which you can use the test.

2 *Research hypothesis*. This states the prediction that the experiment is designed to test.

3 *Sample data*. This gives a table of sample data that can be analysed using the test.

4 *Rationale*. Under this heading the aims of the test are explained and information is provided to help you understand the reasons for accepting or rejecting the null hypothesis.

5 *Step-by-step instructions*. This section goes through a worked example using the sample data with a clear statement of all the steps and calculations you need to carry out when doing the test.

6 *Looking up probabilities in statistical tables*. This section helps you to find your way around statistical tables in order to decide whether the data justify rejecting the null hypothesis.

7 *Conclusions*. This section states the results of the experiment and whether they are significant at a specific level of significance.

 Progress box five

- Non-parametric statistical tests are based on ordinal data.
- Ordinal data are ranked from the lowest score to the highest score.
- There are special rules for assigning tied ranks to identical scores.
- Statistical tests are presented under standard headings.

6 Wilcoxon test (related)

6.1 Scores from same participants

In related designs the same participants do both conditions. Each participant produces a pair of scores, one score for each condition. This makes it possible to make a direct comparison between each participant's scores in the two conditions. Because each participant has a pair of related scores in both conditions, the differences between the pairs of scores can be calculated for each participant.

For the non-parametric Wilcoxon test the recall scores are measured as ordinal data, which can be ranked. Each participant will have a pair of scores, and we can calculate the differences between these pairs of ordinal scores. Once these differences have been calculated, instructions about how these differences can be ranked are given in Section 6.2.

For presenting sets of paired related scores it is a convention to list the participants in the left-hand column. This is to indicate that each participant has a pair of related scores for each condition, as shown in Table 6.1.

We have calculated the differences for participants 1 and 2 in Table 6.1.

? Question 6.1   (a) Calculate the differences for participants 3 and 4 and add these to Table 6.1.

    (b) Calculate the mean scores for the two conditions and add the means to Table 6.1.

Table 6.1   Differences between pairs of related scores

Participants	Condition 1	Condition 2	Differences between scores
1	10	6	4
2	5	2	3
3	4	2	
4	5	2	
Total scores	24	12	
Mean scores			

6.2   Ranking differences between conditions

As we pointed out in Chapter 5, non-parametric tests are based on ordinal data. The differences that were calculated in Table 6.1 were between pairs of scores, measured as ordinal data. This means that the differences themselves are ordinal data and can be ranked.

If you refer back to Chapter 5, Section 5.3 gives instructions about how to assign tied ranks to identical scores. These rules apply just as much to tied ranks in differences between scores. Ranks of the differences between the scores in two conditions are shown in Table 6.2.

In order to rank the differences in the Differences column in Table 6.2 you need to give the lowest rank of 1 to the lowest difference of 2 and the rank of 2 to the next lowest difference of 3.

Note the two highest differences, which are both 4. The rule is to assign the average of the ranks these two differences would have been entitled to. These would have been the two highest ranks of 3 and 4. The average is 3.5 so the two differences of 4 are both allocated tied ranks of 3.5.

Table 6.2   Ranking differences between scores in two conditions

Participants	Condition 1	Condition 2	Differences	Ranks
1	6	2	4	3.5
2	5	3	2	1
3	7	4	3	2
4	7	3	4	3.5

6.3 Ranking plus and minus differences

The next point to consider is the possibility that not all the differences will go in the same positive direction. In all the tables presented so far the differences have always been in the same direction.

Participants may produce variable scores. It is by no means certain that all participants will produce higher scores in Condition 1 than in Condition 2. It is quite likely that one or other of the participants may produce scores that are higher in Condition 2.

It is a convention that the Condition 2 scores are subtracted from the Condition 1 scores. When there are higher scores in Condition 1 the differences will be allocated plus signs. When the scores in Condition 1 are lower than in Condition 2 the differences will be allocated minus signs.

The calculation of plus and minus signed differences is shown in Table 6.3. Participants 1 and 2 had higher scores in Condition 1, but participants 3 and 4 had lower scores in Condition 1 and higher scores in Condition 2. By subtracting Condition 2 scores from Condition 1 scores, participants 1 and 2 have plus differences and the participants 3 and 4 have minus differences.

There is a special rule for ranking plus and minus differences. The rule is that the differences are ranked in order from lowest to highest, completely ignoring the plus and minus differences. In Table 6.3 the lowest difference of +1 is assigned a rank of 1. The next lowest difference of −3 is assigned a rank of 2.

Note that the two highest differences are +5 and −5. The two highest ranks of 3 and 4 are averaged to give tied ranks of 3.5 to both these differences.

Table 6.3   Ranking plus and minus differences

Participants	Condition 1	Condition 2	Differences (1 − 2)	Ranks of differences
1	10	5	+5	3.5
2	8	7	+1	1
3	7	10	−3	2
4	3	8	−5	3.5

6.4 Ties between scores

We have so far discussed applying the usual rules for assigning tied ranks to the plus and minus differences between pairs of scores. In every case it is the differences between pairs of scores in the two conditions that are being ranked.

But this assumes that it is possible to calculate differences between pairs of scores for every participant. There is a different type of tie between pairs of scores that makes it impossible to calculate a difference between the scores in the first place.

This type of tie occurs when the two scores for a particular participant are the same. There is no difference between the pairs of scores in favour of one condition or the other. In Table 6.4 participant 3 has the same score of 7 in both conditions.

With this type of tie between a participant's paired scores on the two conditions, the problem is that there is no basis for deciding whether this participant had a higher score for Condition 1 or Condition 2. The only difference that can be calculated for participant 3 is zero, indicating that there is no difference between the two scores of 7 (shown by the 0 in the Differences column). This lack of difference has to be recorded as a tie. As you can see in Table 6.4, this tie must be ignored as far as the ranking of differences is concerned.

Only four ranks can be assigned to the other four participants, rank 1 for the lowest score of –2, tied ranks of 2.5 for the two scores of +4 and –4, and rank 4 for the highest score of –5.

Table 6.4   Ties between scores

Participants	Condition 1	Condition 2	Differences (1 – 2)	Ranks of differences
1	10	15	–5	4
2	8	10	–2	1
3	7	7	0	(tie)
4	6	2	+4	2.5
5	3	7	–4	2.5

6.5   Selecting a statistical test in the Decision Chart

We will now take you through the answers you need to give in the Decision Chart (inside back cover) in order to select an appropriate statistical test for analysing ordinal data for two conditions in which the same participants do both conditions.

Differences between conditions?
The answer to this question is 'Yes' because the aim of the experiment is to test predicted differences between experimental conditions.

One or two variables?
Follow the line for one variable.

How many experimental conditions?
The answer is two conditions because the experiment is testing differences between two conditions.

Related or unrelated design?
The answer is related design because the same participants are doing both conditions.

Non-parametric or parametric test?
The answer is non-parametric because non-parametric statistical tests are suitable for analysing ranked ordinal data.

If you proceed down the Decision Chart in this way, you will arrive at the Wilcoxon test (related). The Wilcoxon test (related) is the appropriate non-parametric test for a related design with two conditions.

Section 6.6 will provide practical advice about what you have learned so far in this chapter about how to rank positive and negative differences and how to deal with ties between differences and ties between scores.

6.6   Using the Wilcoxon test (related)

When to use

The Wilcoxon test (related) should be used for a related design when the same participants are doing two conditions and the data are ordinal.

Research hypothesis

The experimenter predicted that students would be more relaxed when listening to music and so would recall more words in a music condition than in a condition with no music.

? **Question 6.2**   Is this a one-tailed or a two-tailed hypothesis?

Sample data

All participants learned one list with music and one list without music. To control for order effects, half the participants learned first with music and then without music, while the other half of the particpants did the conditions in the reverse order. Recall scores are shown in Table 6.5.

Table 6.5   Recall scores with and without music

Participants	Condition 1 (without music)	Condition 2 (music)	d	Ranks of d	Signed ranks (plus)	Signed ranks (minus)
1	3	5	−2	5		(−)5
2	4	5	−1	2		(−)2
3	3	2	+1	2	(+)2	
4	1	5	−4	8.5		(−)8.5
5	5	4	+1	2	(+)2	
6	2	5	−3	7		(−)7
7	3	5	−2	5		(−)5
8	4	4	0	(tie)		
9	1	5	−4	8.5		(−)8.5
10	3	5	−2	5		(−)5
Means	2.9	4.5		Rank totals	(+)4	(−)41

Notes on Table 6.5

1 In the *d* column plus and minus differences have been calculated by subtracting scores in Condition 2 from scores in Condition 1.
2 In the Ranks of *d* column ranks have been assigned regardless of the plus and minus differences (note that there are a lot of tied ranks).
3 The ranks of *d* are now assigned to the two columns of Signed ranks (plus) and Signed ranks (minus). The signs are taken from the original signs of the *d* column, but it is the *ranks* that are assigned.
4 The Signed ranks (plus) and Signed ranks (minus) columns are added up separately to give rank totals of +4 and −41, respectively.
5 The smaller rank total of (+)4 represents the value of *W*.

Rationale

The aim of the Wilcoxon test (related) is to compare the number of plus and minus signed ranks in the two conditions. It is possible to calculate the differences in the scores for each participant. If there are only random differences between the conditions, as stated by the null hypothesis, the plus and minus differences will be roughly equal. If there is a preponderance of plus or minus ranks in the predicted direction the null hypothesis can be rejected.

Step-by-step instructions for calculating the value of W

These are given in Box A.

 Box A

Step-by-step instructions for calculating the value of W

1   Calculate the difference (d) between each pair of scores, assigning plus or minus signs.   Subtract Condition 2 from Condition 1: see the d column in Table 6.5.

2   Rank the differences (d) from the smallest (rank 1) to the largest. When ranking *omit* tied scores and *ignore* the plus and minus signs.   See the 'Ranks of d' column in Table 6.5.

3   Assign the ranks of d to the 'Signed ranks' columns based on the ranks in the d column.   See plus and minus signs in 'Signed ranks (plus)' and 'Signed ranks (minus)' columns in Table 6.5.

4   Add the rank totals for signed ranks (plus) and signed ranks (minus) separately.   Rank total (plus) = (+)4
Rank total (minus) = (−)41

5   Take the smaller rank total as W. $W = 4$

6   Note the number of participants N (not counting ties). $N = 10 - 1$ (tie) $= 9$

Looking up the significance of W in Table A

Table A (at the back of the book) gives the probabilities for testing one-tailed and two-tailed hypotheses. The smaller rank total of $W = 4$ has to be equal to or less than the values in Table A. N refers to the number of participants. In our example there were ten participants but only nine showed a difference between the conditions. Participant 8 was a tie and so is omitted from the analysis because the tie cannot be ranked as a plus or a minus. So $N = 9$.

In Table A look along the row for $N = 9$. The calculated W of 4 is smaller than the value of 6 in the second column. If you look at the top of the table the level of significance for a one-tailed test is $p < 0.025$. Since this is a lower probability than the acceptable $p < 0.05$ the null hypothesis can be rejected.

Conclusions

It is essential to look back to the means in Table 6.5 to check whether the difference is in the direction predicted by the one-tailed hypothesis. The means show that participants recall more words when music is playing in Condition 2 than without music in Condition 1 ($p < 0.025$).

 Progress box six

- In related designs pairs of scores in the two conditions are produced by the same participants.
- Differences are calculated between pairs of scores for each participant.
- These differences are ranked following the rules for assigning tied ranks to identical differences.
- Difference rated as plus or minus are ranked regardless of plus or minus signs.
- Ties between a participant's scores in the two conditions, which do not indicate a difference in favour of either condition, are recorded as ties and cannot be ranked.
- Totals of plus and minus ranks are added separately. The lower rank is W.
- The appropriate non-parametric statistical test for analysing related ordinal data for two conditions is the Wilcoxon test (related).

? Question 6.3   A research hypothesis predicted that comprehension scores would be higher for a text with short sentences than long sentences. The results are shown in Table 6.6.

(a) Calculate the mean scores for the two conditions to two decimal places.

(b) Following the step-by-step instructions in Box A, complete the blank columns for *d*, Ranks of *d* and the Signed ranks (plus and minus) in Table 6.6.

(c) Is the smaller *W* significant and, if so, at what level of significance?

Table 6.6 Data for Wilcoxon (related)

Participants	Condition 1 (short sentences)	Condition 2 (long sentences)	d	Ranks of d	Signed ranks (plus)	Signed ranks (minus)
1	7	8				
2	10	6				
3	13	4				
4	8	4				
5	7	7				
6	8	10				
7	6	3				
8	10	3				
Means				Rank totals		

7 Mann–Whitney test (unrelated)

7.1 Scores from different participants

In unrelated designs different participants do each condition. Because different participants do only one condition, it is not possible to compare the scores on both conditions for each participant. Instead all individual scores have to be ranked overall across both conditions.

In Table 7.1 scores are given for each of the conditions. But in this case there is no column for participants. The reason is that the scores in the two conditions are produced by two groups of different participants. We have indicated this by referring to the two different groups who are doing the two conditions.

For the non-parametric Mann–Whitney test the scores are measured as ordinal data, which can be ranked. Instructions about how to rank all the individual scores are given in Section 7.2.

Table 7.1 Scores for two conditions produced by different participants

	Condition 1 Group 1	Condition 2 Group 2
	10	5
	15	6
	25	7
	8	10
Means	14.5	7

? Question 7.1   Is it possible to calculate the differences between the scores in Condition 1 and Condition 2?

7.2   Overall ranking of scores

There is no basis for comparing differences in scores when groups of different participants are doing the two conditions. But it is still necessary to rank the scores in the two conditions in order to see whether there are higher ranks in one condition and lower ranks in the other condition.

The way this is done is to rank all the scores in the two conditions together. The lowest score across the two conditions is assigned a rank of 1, the next lowest gets rank 2, and so on until the highest rank is assigned to the highest score. This results in an overall ranking of all the scores regardless of which scores are in which condition.

The overall ranks for the scores in Table 7.1 are shown in Table 7.2. The lowest score of 5, in Condition 2, is assigned a rank of 1. The next lowest score of 6, also in Condition 2, is assigned a rank of 2. The third lowest score of 7, again in Condition 2, is assigned the next rank of 3. The fourth lowest score of 8, in Condition 1 this time, is assigned a rank of 4.

You will notice that in the overall scores there are two scores of 10. One score of 10 was produced by a participant in Condition 1 and the other score of 10 by a participant in Condition 2. These two scores are assigned tied ranks of 5.5 in the overall ranks.

7.3   Rank totals for each condition

In order to decide whether the ranks are higher for one of the conditions, the totals of ranks are added separately for each condition. The aim is to

Table 7.2   Overall ranking of scores

Condition 1		Condition 2	
Scores	*Ranks*	*Scores*	*Ranks*
10	5.5	5	1
15	7	6	2
25	8	7	3
8	4	10	5.5

check whether the ranks of scores in Condition 1 are higher than the ranks of scores in Condition 2.

To make this absolutely clear, there are two stages in assigning ranks to scores from different participants. The first stage is to carry out an overall ranking of all individual scores across both conditions. The second stage is to add the rank totals for each of the conditions separately.

The totals of the ranks for Condition 1 and Condition 2 are shown in Table 7.3.

In Table 7.1 the means are higher for Condition 1 than for Condition 2. In Table 7.2 the higher scores in Condition 1 have been assigned higher ranks than in Condition 2. In Table 7.3 when the totals of the ranks are added up separately for each condition the total of ranks is higher in Condition 1 than in Condition 2.

These links between higher scores, higher means, higher ranks and higher rank totals in Condition 1 demonstrate the connections between scores and ranks for assessing ordinal data.

Table 7.3   Rank totals for the two conditions

	Condition 1 Ranks	Condition 2 Ranks
	5.5	1
	7	2
	8	3
	4	5.5
Rank totals	24.5	11.5

7.4   Selecting a statistical test in the Decision Chart

We will now take you through the answers you need to give in the Decision Chart (inside back cover) in order to select an appropriate statistical test for analysing ordinal data for two conditions in which two groups of different participants do each condition.

Differences between conditions?
The answer to this question is 'Yes' because the aim of the experiment is to test predicted differences between experimental conditions.

One or two variables?
Follow the line for one variable.

How many experimental conditions?
The answer is two conditions because the experiment is testing differences between two conditions.

Related or unrelated design?
The answer is unrelated design because different participants are doing each condition.

Non-parametric or parametric test?
The answer is non-parametric because non-parametric statistical tests are suitable for analysing ranked ordinal data.

If you proceed down the Decision Chart in this way, you will arrive at the Mann–Whitney test (unrelated). The Mann–Whitney (unrelated) is the appropriate non-parametric test for an unrelated design with two conditions.

Section 7.5 will provide practical advice about what you have learned so far in this chapter about how to rank overall scores and how to calculate rank totals between conditions.

7.5   Using the Mann–Whitney test (unrelated)

When to use

The Mann–Whitney test (unrelated) should be used for an unrelated design when different participants are doing two conditions and the data are ordinal.

Research hypothesis

The prediction was that a group of participants who are given a relevant title before learning a text would recall the text better than a group of participants given no title.

? Question 7.2   Why is it better to use different participants in each condition to test this hypothesis?

Sample data

One group of participants was given a relevant title before reading a text (Condition 2). A second group of participants was given no title before reading the text (Condition 1). Participants in both groups were tested for their memory of the text. The results are shown in Table 7.4.

Table 7.4 Recall scores for texts with and without a title

Condition 1 (no title)	*Overall ranks (ranks 1)*	*Condition 2 (title)*	*Overall ranks (ranks 2)*
3	3	9	13
4	4	7	10.5
2	1.5	5	6
6	8.5	10	14
2	1.5	6	8.5
5	6	8	12
		5	6
		7	10.5
Rank totals	$T_1 = 24.5$		$T_2 = 80.5$
Means 3.67		7.13	

Notes on Table 7.4

1 The overall ranks 1 and 2 are the result of an overall ranking of all scores.
2 The rank totals (T_1 and T_2) have been added up separately for each condition.
3 Note that there are different numbers of participants in each group, 6 participants in Condition 1 and 8 participants in Condition 2.

Rationale

The aim of the Mann–Whitney test (unrelated) is to compare the rank totals in the two conditions based on an overall ranking. If the ranked differences between conditions are random, as stated by the null hypothesis, there should be roughly equal ranks in the two conditions. If there is a large preponderance of low or high ranks in one condition in the predicted direction, the differences between the rank totals for the two conditions will justify the rejection of the null hypothesis..

Step-by-step instructions for calculating the value of U

These are given in Box B.

■ **Box B**

Step-by-step instructions for calculating the value of U

1 Rank *all* the scores (taking both groups together as an *overall* set of ranks), giving rank 1 to the lowest score in the usual way.

See overall ranks for both conditions taken together in Table 7.4.

2 After ranking all the scores, add the rank totals for each condition.

$T_1 = 24.5$
$T_2 = 80.5$

3 Calculate U using the formula:

$$U = n_1 n_2 + \frac{n_1(n_1 + 1)}{2} - T_1$$

$$U = 6 \times 8 + \frac{6(6 + 1)}{2} - 24.5$$

$$= 48 + \frac{42}{2} - 24.5$$

$$= 48 + 21 - 24.5$$

$$= 44.5$$

n_1 = number of participants in Condition 1

$n_1 = 6$

n_2 = number of participants in Condition 2

$n_2 = 8$

T_1 = rank total for Condition 1

$T_1 = 24.5$

4 Next substitute the values of U, n_1 and n_2 in the following formula and calculate U':

$$U' = n_1 n_2 - U$$

$$U' = 6 \times 8 - 44.5$$

$$= 3.5$$

5 Take the smaller value of U or U' as U.

$U = 3.5$

The formula for U in step 3 may look rather daunting. All that is happening is that U has to take into account the unequal number of participants in each group (n_1 and n_2). The convention is to subtract T_1 from the formula.

Looking up the significance of *U* in Table B

Tables B(1) and B(2) give the probabilities for testing one-tailed and two-tailed hypotheses. It may seem odd to have to look up *U* in two separate tables. The reason is that the tables provide the *U* values for different significance levels. Table B(1) gives the probabilities for a one-tailed hypothesis at $p < 0.05$. Table B(2) gives the probabilities for $p < 0.01$ (one-tailed) and $p < 0.02$ (two-tailed). The smaller value of *U* has to be equal to or less than the values in Table B.

Looking at Table B(1) first, the number of participants in Condition 1 ($n_1 = 6$) is listed along the top row and the number of participants in Condition 2 ($n_2 = 8$) is listed in the left-hand column. Locate 6 along the top and 8 down the column. Where these two meet the value of *U* is 10. Our calculated *U* of 3.5 is smaller than this so the null hypothesis can be rejected. Looking at Table B(2) the *U* of 3.5 is also smaller than the value of 6 for $n_1 = 6$ and $n_2 = 8$. The null hypothesis for a one-tailed hypothesis can be rejected ($p < 0.01$).

Conclusions

It is essential to refer back to the means in Table 7.4 to check whether the results are significant in the predicted direction. The means show a difference in favour of Condition 2 (title). It can be concluded that the prediction that participants will recall more of a text when given an appropriate title was supported ($p < 0.01$).

 Progress box seven

- In unrelated designs the scores in the two conditions are produced by different participants.
- Individual scores are assigned an overall ranking across both conditions.
- Totals of ranks are added separately for each condition.
- The appropriate non-parametric statistical test for analysing unrelated ordinal data for two conditions is the Mann–Whitney test (unrelated).

? Question 7.3   An experimenter predicted that words presented on the left-hand side of a screen would be recognized more quickly because of the direction of reading left to right in English compared with words presented on the right-hand side. The measure was the time taken to recognize the words. The data are given in Table 7.5.

Table 7.5   Data for Mann–Whitney (unrelated)

Left-hand presentation	Overall ranks (ranks 1)	Right-hand presentation	Overall ranks (ranks 2)
9		8	
3		5	
2		7	
6		20	
1		11	
5		6	
Rank totals	$T_1 =$		$T_2 =$

(a) Following steps 1 and 2 in **Box B**, first calculate the overall ranks of scores in Table 7.5 and add them on the overall ranks columns.

(b) Add the rank totals separately for each condition.

(c) Do the rank totals support the research hypothesis? (Remember that lower rank totals represent quicker recognition times.)

8 Introduction to parametric *t* tests

8.1 Comparisons between parametric and non-parametric tests

The parametric *t* tests, which we will be introducing in this chapter, are designed to test differences between two conditions. In this way, they are like the non-parametric tests for two conditions that were discussed in Chapters 6 and 7. In other ways, parametric tests and non-parametric tests are quite different.

We will start by emphasizing the similarities. In both cases the tests analyse differences between two experimental conditions. The research hypothesis predicts that there will be differences between the two experimental conditions.

Another similarity between parametric *t* tests and non-parametric tests is that they use similar methods for analysing data from the same participants and data from groups of different participants.

Chapter 6 described the way in which the non-parametric Wilcoxon test (related) deals with data from a related design, when the same participants do both experimental conditions. Participants who do both experimental conditions produce pairs of scores for the two conditions. This means that for each participant it is possible to calculate the differences between scores in the two conditions.

The parametric *t* test (related) also compares differences between pairs of scores on two conditions for each participant.

Chapter 7 described the way in which the non-parametric Mann–Whitney test (unrelated) deals with data from an unrelated design, when groups of different participants do each of the experimental conditions. Because a different group of participants does each of the conditions, it is not possible to compare differences between scores. Instead all the scores have to be dealt with as individual scores.

The parametric *t* test (unrelated) also assumes that there is no basis for comparing scores directly. The aim is to investigate whether the mean of the scores for the group of participants doing one condition is higher than the mean of the scores for the different group of participants who are doing the other condition.

The major differences between the two types of statistical tests arise from the different way in which the data are measured.

Non-parametric tests are based on ordinal data in which scores can be ordered from the lowest score to the highest score. Scores can be ranked, giving the lowest rank to the lowest score and so on until the highest rank is assigned to the highest score.

Parametric *t* tests are based on interval data. Interval data are so called because the intervals between scores are considered to be equal. This makes it possible to carry out numerical calculations instead of simply ranking the scores.

8.2 Numerical calculations for parametric tests

One of the most common numerical calculations for parametric tests is to square numbers and to add the squared numbers in various combinations.

Squaring a number simply means multiplying a number by itself. You will probably remember from your school days that when you calculate the squares of positive and minus scores you always end up with positive numbers. For example:

$$3 \times 3 = +9$$
$$-3 \times -3 = +9$$

? Question 8.1 Calculate the squares of the following numbers.

(a) 5

(b) −5

(c) −1

(d) 3

The next step is to add up squared numbers to arrive at a total of the squared numbers. Another word for total is sum. The term used is *sum of squares* (SS). The symbol for sum is Σ. This symbol is the Greek letter for S (pronounced 'sigma').

It is a general principle for parametric tests that variance is calculated by squaring numbers and summing them in various combinations. You will be given detailed step-by-step instructions for each parametric test about which numbers should be squared and summed.

8.3   Calculating variances

Based on the numerical calculations that can be carried out on interval data, it is possible to calculate precise amounts of variability in participants' scores. The calculated differences in scores between the two conditions can be compared with the total amount of variability in scores.

When using parametric *t* tests the usual term for describing variability is *variance*. Variance represents calculated estimates of variability in scores.

Predicted variance represents the predicted differences in scores between the two conditions.

Total variance represents all the variability in scores, including the variance due to predicted differences and irrelevant differences between individual participants.

8.4   Ratio of variances

Another way of expressing the comparison between predicted variance and total variance is as a ratio between the two types of variance.

The first type of variance is the predicted variance. The prediction is that there will be differences between two conditions as a result of the independent variable selected by the researcher.

The second type of variance is total variance. This is the result of all the variables affecting participants' performance. Total variance includes the variance caused by the predicted independent variable, as well as unpredicted variance due to individual differences between participants and the effects of irrelevant variables.

The comparison between these two types of variance can be expressed as a ratio:

$$\frac{\text{Predicted variance due to independent variable}}{\text{Total variance due to all variables}}$$

Parametric *t* tests test whether the predicted variance is large enough to result in a high ratio of variance in which the predicted variance between two conditions is relatively large in comparison with the total variance.

As we shall see, it is the concept of a ratio between predicted and total variance that underlies all parametric statistical tests. You do not need to worry too much about this now, but you will come across this ratio when the *t* tests are described. Full details about the implications of predicted and total variance will be given in the description of the *t* tests in the next two chapters.

 Progress box eight

- Parametric *t* tests are similar to non-parametric tests for testing differences between two experimental conditions.
- Both parametric *t* tests and non-parametric tests distinguish between related and unrelated designs.
- Parametric tests are different from non-parametric tests because they require interval data, which provide the basis for numerical calculations.
- Ratios of variances compare predicted variance with total variance.

9 *t* test (related)

9.1 Scores from same participants

In related designs the same participants do both conditions. Each participant produces a pair of scores, one score for Condition 1 and one score for Condition 2.

This makes it possible to make a direct comparison between each participant's scores in the two conditions. Each participant has a pair of related scores in both conditions so the differences between the scores can be calculated for each participant.

Because the *t* test (related) is based on pairs of related scores, another name for the *t* test (related) is the paired *t* test.

9.2 Squaring differences

You should remember from Chapter 8 that one of the most common numerical calculations used for interval data is to square numbers and add them to produce sums of squares. For related designs it is the differences between conditions that are squared.

Table 9.1 shows the plus and minus differences between the scores on

Table 9.1 Squares of differences between conditions

Participants	Condition 1	Condition 2	Differences d *(1 − 2)*	Squares of differences (d²)
1	10	5	+5	25
2	8	7	+1	1
3	7	10	−3	9
4	3	8	−5	25

two conditions, obtained by subtracting the scores for Condition 2 from the scores in Condition 1.

For the *t* test (related) each plus or minus difference is squared. The squares of both the plus or minus differences are always a positive number.

The next step is to find the totals of the scores, the differences and the sum of squared differences, as shown in Table 9.2.

Table 9.2 Totals (sums) of differences and squared differences

Participants	Condition 1	Condition 2	Differences d *(1 – 2)*	Squares of differences *(d²)*
1	10	5	+5	25
2	8	7	+1	1
3	7	10	−3	9
4	3	8	−5	25
Totals (sums)	28	30	−2	60

? Question 9.1 Using the totals for each condition, calculate the mean for each condition in Table 9.2.

Note that the total of the differences takes into account the plus and minus differences ($+6 - 8 = -2$).

The sum of positive squares always results in a positive number (here 60).

9.3 Ratio of variances

The predicted variance is measured as the sum of differences between the scores in the two conditions. The research hypothesis predicts differences between two experimental conditions as a result of the independent variable selected by the experimenter.

The predicted variance has to be compared with the total variance in scores. Total variance is measured using the sum of squared differences between the two conditions for all participants.

The *t* test (related) calculates a ratio between the predicted variance and the total variance.

9.4   Selecting a statistical test in the Decision Chart

Differences between conditions?
The answer to this question is 'Yes' because the aim of the experiment is to test predicted differences between experimental conditions.

One or two variables?
Follow the line for one variable.

How many experimental conditions?
The answer is two conditions because the experiment is testing differences between two conditions.

Related or unrelated design?
The answer is related design because the same participants are doing both conditions.

Non-parametric or parametric test?
The answer is parametric because parametric statistical tests are suitable for analysing numerical interval data.

You will find that if you answered the above four questions in the Decision Chart (inside back cover) as suggested, you will arrive at the *t* test (related). The *t* test (related) is the appropriate parametric test for a related design with two conditions.

9.5   Using the *t* test (related)

When to use

The *t* test (related) should be used for a related design when the same participants are doing two conditions and the data are interval.

Research hypothesis

The experimenter predicted that participants would recall more words from a simple text than from a complex text.

? Question 9.2   Is this a one-tailed or a two-tailed hypothesis?

Sample data

All participants were given 2 minutes to read a simple text and a complex text and after 10 minutes they were asked to recall the words. To counterbalance possible order effects of doing both conditions, half of the participants were presented with the simple text first and the other half with the complex text first. The results are shown in Table 9.3.

Table 9.3 Recall scores for simple and complex texts

Participants	Condition 1 (simple text)	Condition 2 (complex text)	d	d²
1	10	2	8	64
2	5	1	4	16
3	6	7	−1	1
4	3	4	−1	1
5	9	4	5	25
6	8	5	3	9
7	7	2	5	25
8	5	5	0	0
9	6	3	3	9
10	5	4	1	1
			$\Sigma d = 27$	$\Sigma d^2 = 151$
Means	6.4	3.7		

Notes on Table 9.3
1 The differences (*d*) are calculated by subtracting the scores in Condition 2 from the scores in Condition 1.
2 The sum of differences (Σd) is calculated taking into account the plus and minus signs (predicted variance).
3 The sum of the squares of differences (Σd^2) is calculated by adding the positive squares (total variance).

Rationale

When the same participants are used for both conditions, the predicted variance is calculated as the sum of the differences between the scores in both conditions. The predicted variance between conditions is expressed as a proportion of total variance. If there are only random differences between the scores in the two conditions, as stated by the null hypothesis, the variance due to the predicted differences would be relatively small in relation to the total variance in scores. In this case the null hypothesis cannot be rejected.

Step-by-step instructions for calculating t (related)

These are given in Box C.

 Box C

Step-by-step instructions for calculating t (related)

1   Calculate the differences between participants' scores by subtracting Condition 2 scores from Condition 1.

   See column d in Table 9.3.

2   Sum differences, taking into account pluses and minuses.

   $\Sigma d = 27$

3   Square the differences.

   See column d^2 in Table 9.3.

4   Sum the squared differences.

   $\Sigma d^2 = 151$

5   Square the total of differences.

   $(\Sigma d^2) = 27 \times 27 = 729$

6   Find the total number of participants.

   $N = 10$

7   Find t from the formula:

$$t = \frac{\Sigma d}{\sqrt{\dfrac{N\Sigma d^2 - (\Sigma d)^2}{N-1}}}$$

$$t = \frac{27}{\sqrt{\dfrac{10 \times 151 - (27)^2}{10-1}}}$$

$$= \frac{27}{\sqrt{\dfrac{1510 - 729}{9}}}$$

$$= \frac{27}{\sqrt{86.78}}$$

$\sqrt{}$ = take the square root

$$= \frac{27}{9.315}$$

$$= 2.89$$

8   Calculate the degrees of freedom.

   $df = N - 1 = 10 - 1 = 9$

Notes on calculations in Box C

1 Look carefully at the definitions of symbols in Box C and follow the calculations on the right-hand side of the box. Note that you also have to calculate the square of the total differences ($27 \times 27 = 729$).

2 In the main formula in step 7 the sum of the differences between pairs of scores (Σd) represents the predicted differences between the conditions (on the top line of the formula).

3 The equation on the bottom line of the formula represents total variance in terms of sums of squares. The whole formula represents a ratio between predicted variance and total variance.

4 In step 8 you are asked to calculate the degrees of freedom (df). Take it on trust that df equals the number of participants (N) minus 1. In our example $df = 10 - 1 = 9$. We will be explaining the principles of degrees of freedom in a later chapter.

5 The calculations in Box C will be much easier if you invest in a calculator which has a sum of squares button (Σx^2) which automatically works out squares and adds them up. If you have a calculator with memory you can put each square into memory and record the total sum of squares. A square root button is essential to complete the last instruction to 'take the square root'.

Looking up the significance of the *t* test (related) in Table C

Table C is the appropriate table for the *t* test for two conditions, whether the *t* test is related or unrelated. Table C gives the probabilities for the values of *t*. The calculated *t* has to be equal to or larger than the values in Table C. You need to use the df (in our example $df = 10 - 1 = 9$).

To find the value of *t* look along the row for $df = 9$. The value of *t* for ($p < 0.05$) for a one-tailed hypothesis is 1.833. Our calculated *t* of 2.89 in Box C is larger than this value. In fact, looking along the $df = 9$ row the calculated *t* is larger than the value of 2.821 for $p < 0.01$ for a one-tailed hypothesis. The null hypothesis can be rejected ($p < 0.01$).

Conclusions

It is essential to look at the means in Table 9.3 to check whether any significant differences are in the predicted direction. The means in Table 9.3 show that the results are significant in the predicted direction, supporting the one-tailed hypothesis that more words are recalled from a simple text than from a complex text ($p < 0.01$).

Progress box nine

- In related designs pairs of scores in the two conditions are produced by the same participants.
- The total of differences is calculated between the pairs of scores for each participant. This represents predicted variance.
- In order to calculate total variance the squares of differences are added to produce a sum of squares.
- The appropriate parametric statistical test for calculating a ratio between predicted and total variance when analysing related interval data for two conditions is the *t* test (related).

? Question 9.3

(a) Using the data in Table 9.4, calculate the means for the two conditions.

(b) Calculate the plus and minus differences (*d*) between the two conditions (Condition 1 – Condition 2) and insert these in the *d* column in Table 9.4.

(c) Square the differences and insert these in the d^2 column.

(d) Calculate the sum of differences (Σd), taking into account plus and minus differences.

(e) Calculate the sum of squares (Σd^2).

Table 9.4   Data for *t* test (related)

Participants	Condition 1	Condition 2	d	d^2
1	6	2		
2	7	1		
3	8	3		
4	10	4		
5	8	3		
6	8	2		
7	5	7		
8	3	4		
Means			$\Sigma d =$	$\Sigma d^2 =$

10 *t* test (unrelated)

In unrelated designs different groups of participants do each condition. Because different participants do only one of the experimental conditions, the scores in the two conditions are unrelated. It is not possible to compare scores in both conditions for each participant.

Instead all scores have to be dealt with as invidual scores. The *t* test (unrelated) is based on comparing the means for the two groups doing each condition. This is because there is no basis for comparing differences between related pairs of scores for each participant.

Because the *t* test (unrelated) is based on unrelated scores for two conditions, which are independent of each other, another name for the *t* test (unrelated) is the independent *t* test.

10.2 Squaring scores

You should remember from Chapter 8 that one of the most common numerical calculations used for parametric tests is to square numbers and add them to produce sums of squares.

For unrelated designs all the individual scores are squared. An example is given in Table 10.1.

To make it clear that different groups are doing the two conditions, Table 10.1 shows Group 1 doing Condition 1 and Group 2 doing Condition 2.

? Question 10.1 Do the scores of 5 in Condition 1 and Condition 2 in Table 10.1 represent tied scores?

Table 10.1 Squares of individual scores

Group 1 Condition 1		Group 2 Condition 2	
Scores	*Squares*	*Scores*	*Squares*
2	4	4	16
5	25	5	25
4	16	3	9
3	9	6	36

The next step is to add the totals of the scores and the sums of squares separately for Condition 1 and Condition 2. These totals of scores and squares are shown in Table 10.2.

Table 10.2 Sums of scores and squares

	Group 1 Condition 1		Group 2 Condition 2	
	Scores	*Squares*	*Scores*	*Squares*
	2	4	4	16
	5	25	5	25
	4	16	3	9
	3	9	6	36
Totals (sums)	14	54	18	86
Means	3.5		4.5	

10.3 Ratio of variances

The predicted variance is based on the difference between the means for the two conditions. The research hypothesis predicts differences between two experimental conditions as a result of the independent variable selected by the experimenter.

The predicted variance has to be compared with the total variance in scores. Total variance is based on all the scores produced by participants. Total variance is measured using the sums of squares of scores in each of the two conditions.

The *t* test (unrelated) calculates a ratio between the predicted variance and the total variance.

10.4   Selecting a statistical test in the Decision Chart

Differences between conditions?
The answer to this question is 'Yes' because the aim of the experiment is to test predicted differences between experimental conditions.

One or two variables?
Follow the line for one variable.

How many experimental conditions?
The answer is two conditions because the experiment is testing differences between two conditions.

Related or unrelated design?
The answer is unrelated design because different participants are doing each condition.

Non-parametric or parametric test?
The answer is parametric because parametric statistical tests are suitable for analysing numerical interval data.

You will find that if you answered the above four questions in the Decision Chart (inside back cover) as suggested, you will arrive at the *t* test (unrelated). The *t* test (unrelated) is the appropriate parametric test for an unrelated design with two conditions.

10.5   Using the *t* test (unrelated)

When to use

The *t* test (unrelated) should be used for an unrelated design when different participants are doing two conditions and the data are interval.

Research hypothesis

The experimenter predicted that more words would be recalled from a simple text than from a complex text.

Sample data

Two groups of different participants were used for each condition. One group was asked to read a simple text and the other group of different participants was given a complex text. Both groups were given 2 minutes to read the text and after 10 minutes were asked to recall the words. The results are shown in Table 10.3.

Table 10.3 Recall scores for simple and complex texts

	Condition 1 (simple text)		Condition 2 (complex text)	
	Scores (x_1)	Squared scores (x_1^2)	Scores (x_2)	Squared scores (x_2^2)
	10	100	2	4
	5	25	1	1
	6	36	7	49
	3	9	4	16
	9	81	4	16
	8	64	5	25
	7	49	2	4
	5	25	5	25
	6	36	3	9
	5	25	4	16
	$\sum x_1 = 64$	$\sum x_1^2 = 450$	$\sum x_2 = 37$	$\sum x_2^2 = 165$
Means	$M_1 = 6.4$		$M_2 = 3.7$	

Notes on Table 10.3
1 The means are calculated for Condition 1 and Condition 2.
2 The individual scores are squared.
3 The sums of squares are summed separately for each group of participants.

Rationale

When different participants are used for each condition, the predicted variance is calculated as the difference between the means in the two conditions. The predicted variance is expressed as a proportion of total variance. If there are only random differences between the scores in the two conditions, as stated by the null hypothesis, the variance due to the predicted differences between conditions would be relatively small in relation to the total variance in scores. In this case the null hypothesis cannot be rejected.

Step-by-step instructions for calculating t (unrelated)

These are given in Box D.

Box D

Step-by-step instructions for calculating *t* (unrelated)

1   Sum the totals of scores for each condition (see Table 10.3) and square these.

$(\Sigma x_1)^2 = 64 \times 64 = 4096$
$(\Sigma x_2)^2 = 37 \times 37 = 1369$

2   Calculate the means for each condition.

$M_1 = 6.4$
$M_2 = 3.7$

3   Square the individual scores for each condition.

See columns for squared scores in Table 10.3.

4   Sum the squared scores for each condition separately.

$\Sigma x_1^2 = 450$
$\Sigma x_2^2 = 165$

5   Take the number of participants in each condition

$n_1 = 10$
$n_2 = 10$

6   Calculate the value of *t* using the formula

$$t = \frac{M_1 - M_2}{\sqrt{\dfrac{\left(\Sigma x_1^2 - \dfrac{(\Sigma x_1)^2}{n_1}\right) + \left(\Sigma x_2^2 - \dfrac{(\Sigma x_2)^2}{n_2}\right)}{(n_1 - 1) + (n_2 - 1)}\left(\dfrac{1}{n_1} + \dfrac{1}{n_2}\right)}}$$

$$t = \frac{6.4 - 3.7}{\sqrt{\dfrac{\left(450 - \dfrac{4096}{10}\right) + \left(165 - \dfrac{1369}{10}\right)}{9 + 9}\left(\dfrac{1}{10} + \dfrac{1}{10}\right)}}$$

$$= \frac{2.7}{\sqrt{\dfrac{(450 - 409.6) + (165 - 136.9)}{18} \times \dfrac{1}{5}}}$$

$$= \frac{2.7}{\sqrt{3.806 \times 0.2}}$$

$$= \frac{2.7}{\sqrt{0.7612}}$$

$$= 3.096$$

(*N.B.* It does not matter whether subtracting M_2 from M_1 results in a plus or minus number. When looking up the value of *t* simply ignore the sign).

7   Calculate the degrees of freedom by subtracting 1 from the number of participants in each condition and adding together the results.

$n_1 - 1 = 9$
$n_2 - 1 = 9$
$df = 9 + 9 = 18$

Notes on calculations in Box D

1 Look carefully at the definitions of symbols in Box D and follow the calculations on the right-hand side of the box.

2 In the main formula in step 6 the difference between the means ($M_1 - M_2$) represents the predicted differences between the conditions (on the top line of the formula).

3 The equation on the bottom line of the formula represents total variance in terms of sums of squares. The reason for the horrendous-looking equation on the bottom line is that variances have to be calculated separately for each group of participants and then added to give total variance. All this will seem less formidable (we hope!) as you work your way through the formula. The whole formula represents a ratio between predicted variance and total variance.

4 In step 7 you are asked to calculate the degrees of freedom (df). The special feature of the df for unrelated designs is that you have to subtract 1 from the number of participants in each group (n_1 and n_2). If there are 10 participants in each group then the df for n_1 are $10 - 1 = 9$. The df for n_2 are $10 - 1 = 9$. Adding these two together, $df = 18$. Follow the instructions in Box D. You will be given full details about calculating the df in a later chapter.

5 It is possible to do these calculations on a calculator with a square root button and a memory store. There are also computer programs that will carry out all the calculations automatically, including significance levels. But it is worth following the steps in Box D in order to understand the rationale for the t test (unrelated).

Looking up the significance of the *t* test (unrelated) in Table C

Table C is the appropriate table for the t test for two conditions, whether the t test is related or unrelated. Table C gives the probabilities for the values of t. The calculated t has to be equal to or larger than the values in Table C. You need to use the df (in our example $df = n_1 - 1 + n_2 - 1 = 18$).

To find the value of t look along the row for $df = 18$. The value of t for $p < 0.05$ for a one-tailed hypothesis is 1.734. Our calculated t of 3.096 in Box D is larger than this value. In fact, looking along the $df = 18$ row, the calculated t is larger than the critical value of 2.878 for $p < 0.005$. This is a very small probability of random differences in scores. The null hypothesis can be rejected ($p < 0.005$).

Conclusions

It is essential to look at the means in Table 10.3 to check whether any significant differences are in the predicted direction. This is especially important if a computer program has been used. The means in Table 10.3 show that the results are significant in the predicted direction, supporting the one-tailed hypothesis that more words are recalled from a simple text than from a complex text ($p < 0.005$).

 Progress box ten

- In unrelated designs the scores in the two conditions are produced by different participants.
- Means are calculated for the two conditions. This represents predicted variance.
- In order to calculate total variance the squares of scores for each condition are added to produce sums of squares.
- The appropriate parametric statistical test for calculating a ratio between predicted and total variance when analysing unrelated interval data for two conditions is the *t* test (unrelated).

11 Friedman test (related)

11.1 Scores from same participants for three conditions

We will now be returning to non-parametric tests, this time for three (or more) conditions. The Friedman test is for related designs in which the same participants do all the experimental conditions. As with the statistical tests for two conditions, we are introducing first the simpler non-parametric tests for dealing with three conditions.

The Friedman test (related) is used when the same participants do all three conditions. Each participant produces three scores, one in each of the three conditions. This makes it possible to make a direct comparison between each participant's three scores in all the conditions.

The scores in the conditions are related. But, because there are three conditions it is not possible to calculate the differences between two conditions, as we did for the two conditions in the Wilcoxon test (related) and the *t* test (related). A different kind of ranking has be carried out for three conditions.

An example is given in Table 11.1 of an experiment in which participants are presented with three conditions: lists of very rare words (Condition 1), fairly common words (Condition 2) and very common

Table 11.1 Recall scores for different types of word lists

Participants	Condition 1 (rare words)	Condition 2 (common words)	Condition 3 (very common words)
1	2	3	4
2	3	5	7
3	1	7	4
4	2	6	7

words (Condition 3). Because the conditions are done by the same participants there are three scores for each participant.

11.2   Ranking three conditions

The next step is to rank the scores in Table 11.1. The aim of ranking ordinal data is to test whether participants have higher scores in some conditions than in other conditions. If you look at the scores in Table 11.1 for three conditions you will realize that it is not possible to calculate differences between pairs of scores. But we still need to be able to compare the three scores produced by each participant.

The way the three scores in each of the conditions are ranked may seem rather bizarre but there is a good rationale for it. The three scores for each participant are ranked horizontally across the three related conditions. The aim of ranking the three scores for each participant is that it provides information about whether each participant produced higher or lower scores in the three related conditions.

The three conditions in Table 11.1 are repeated in Table 11.2 but with horizontal ranks for the three related scores in the three conditions for each participant added in the Ranks columns.

Table 11.2   Horizontal ranks of three related scores

Participants	Condition 1		Condition 2		Condition 3	
	Scores	Ranks	Scores	Ranks	Scores	Ranks
1	2	1	3	2	4	3
2	3	1	5	2	7	3
3	1	1	7	3	4	2
4	2	1	6	2	7	3

Notes on Table 11.2
1 The top horizontal row of ranks for participant 1 shows that the score of 2 in Condition 1 is the lowest of the three scores and so is assigned a rank of 1. The score of 3 in Condition 2 is the next lowest score and gets a rank of 2. The score of 4 in Condition 3 is the highest of the three scores for participant 1 and so is assigned the highest rank of 3.
2 If you look at the scores and ranks in Table 11.2 for Participant 2, the scores and ranks are in the same rank order as for Participant 2.
3 Participant 3 is slightly the odd one out. The lowest score of 1 and rank 1 was for Condition 1. But this participant obtained a higher recall score of 7 for Condition 2 compared with a score of 4 for Condition 3.

This participant recalled more words from the list of fairly common words in Condition 2 than the very common words in Condition 3. So the ranks for participant 3 are in the order 1, 3, 2.

11.3   Assigning tied ranks

As is always the case when ranking ordinal data, sometimes there will be identical scores. These are dealt with in the normal way by assigning the average of the ranks they would have been entitled to. An example is given in Table 11.3.

Look at the top row for participant 1. There are two scores of 2. Tied ranks of 1.5 are allocated to these two scores. The score of 4 in Condition 3 is assigned the next available rank of 3.

Table 11.3   Tied ranks

Participants	Condition 1		Condition 2		Condition 3	
	Scores	Ranks	Scores	Ranks	Scores	Ranks
1	2	1.5	2	1.5	4	3
2	3	1	5	2	7	3
3	1	1	7	3	4	2
4	2	1	6	2	7	3

? Question 11.1 Insert the three horizontal ranks for the related scores for participants 5 and 6 in the Ranks columns.

Participants	Condition 1		Condition 2		Condition 3	
	Scores	Ranks	Scores	Ranks	Scores	Ranks
5	3		7		5	
6	3		3		6	

11.4 Rank totals

After having ranked the three related scores horizontally for the three conditions, the next step is to add up the totals of ranks separately for each condition. The idea is to test whether there is a preponderance of higher or lower ranks in any of the three conditions. Taking the data in Table 11.3, the total of ranks for each condition is shown in Table 11.4.

The ranks have been added separately for each condition to produce a total of ranks for each condition. The rank totals are 4.5 for Condition 1, 8.5 for Condition 2 and 11 for Condition 3. As predicted, fewer very rare words were recalled in Condition 1 and most words recalled for the very common words in Condition 3.

Table 11.4 Rank totals

Participants	Condition 1 (rare words)		Condition 2 (common words)		Condition 3 (very common words)	
	Scores	Ranks	Scores	Ranks	Scores	Ranks
1	2	1.5	2	1.5	4	3
2	3	1	5	2	7	3
3	1	1	7	3	4	2
4	2	1	6	2	7	3
Totals	8	4.5	20	8.5	22	11

? **Question 11.2**

(a) Use the totals of scores for each condition in Table 11.4 to calculate the means for each of the three conditions.

(b) Do the means support the prediction that more very common words are recalled (Condition 3) than very rare words (Condition 1)?

The Friedman test (related) can deal with three or more conditions. If there were four conditions there would be four related scores to be ranked horizontally for each participant. Four related scores would be allocated four horizontal ranks, from rank 1 for the lowest score to rank 4 for the highest score.

11.5   Selecting a statistical test in the Decision Chart

Differences between conditions?
The answer to this question is 'Yes' because the aim of the experiment is to test predicted differences between experimental conditions.

One or two variables?
Follow the line for one variable.

How many experimental conditions?
The answer is three or more conditions because the experiment is testing differences between three (or more) conditions.

Related or unrelated design?
The answer is related design because the same participants are doing all conditions.

Non-parametric or parametric test?
The answer is non-parametric because non-parametric statistical tests are suitable for analysing ranked ordinal data.

You will find that if you answered the above four questions in the Decision Chart (inside back cover) as suggested, you will arrive at the Friedman test (related). The Friedman test (related) is the appropriate non-parametric test for a related design with three or more conditions.

11.6   Using the Friedman test (related)

When to use

The Friedman test (related) should be used for a related design when the same participants are doing three or more conditions and the data are ordinal.

Research hypothesis

The experimenter predicted that children would rate some illustrations as being more appealing than other illustrations.

Sample data

A publisher producing a series of children's books wants to choose from three types of illustrations the one which is most appealing to children.

Eight children are asked to rate all three illustrations on a five-point scale. The children were presented with the three illustrations in different orders. The rating scores for the three illustrations are shown in Table 11.5.

Table 11.5 Rating scores for three illustrations

	Condition 1 (illustration A)		Condition 2 (illustration B)		Condition 3 (illustration C)	
Participants	Rating scores	Ranks	Rating scores	Ranks	Rating scores	Ranks
1	2	1	5	3	4	2
2	1	1	5	3	3	2
3	3	1	5	2.5	5	2.5
4	3	2	5	3	2	1
5	2	1	3	2	5	3
6	1	1	4	2.5	4	2.5
7	5	3	3	2	2	1
8	1	1	4	3	3	2
Rank totals		11		21		16
Means	2.25		4.25		3.50	

Notes on Table 11.5
1 Each row of ranks represents the horizontal ranks for the three related scores for the three conditions for each participant.
2 You will notice that some of the ranked scores are the same and are assigned the average of the tied ranks they would have been entitled to.
3 The rank totals for each condition are added to produce rank totals for each of the three conditions.

Rationale

The aim of the Friedman test (related) is to test whether the rank totals are different for the three conditions. If there are random differences between the rank totals for all three conditions, as stated by the null hypothesis, the rank totals would be approximately equal, because there would be equal numbers of low and high ranks in each of the conditions. If the rank totals show a preponderance of high ranks or low ranks in one or other of the conditions, the null hypothesis can be rejected.

Step-by-step instructions for carrying out the Friedman test (related)

These are given in Box E.

 Box E

Step-by-step instructions for calculating the value of χ_r^2

1. Rank the scores for each *separate* participant *horizontally across* each row, giving 1 to the smallest score, 2 to the next score and 3 to the highest score.

   See 'Ranks' columns in Table 11.5 allocating ranks 1, 2, 3 for each participant (sometimes tied, e.g. 2.5 for participants 3 and 6).

2. Calculate the rank totals for each condition.

   $T_1 = 11$, $T_2 = 21$, $T_3 = 16$

3. Note the following symbols:

   number of conditions (C) $C = 3$

   number of participants (N) $N = 8$

   T^2 = squares of rank totals.

   $T^2{}_1 = 11 \times 11 = 121$

   $T^2{}_2 = 21 \times 21 = 441$

   $T^2{}_3 = 16 \times 16 = 256$

   $\sum T^2 = 11^2 + 21^2 + 16^2 = 818$

4. Calculate the value of χ_r^2 using the formula

   $$\chi_r^2 = \left[\frac{12}{NC(C+1)} \sum T^2 \right] - 3N(C+1)$$

   $$\chi_r^2 = \left[\left(\frac{12}{(8 \times 3)(3+1)} \right) (11^2 + 21^2 + 16^2) \right] - 3 \times 8(3+1)$$

   $$= \left[\left(\frac{12}{24 \times 4} \right) (121 + 441 + 256) \right] - (24 \times 4)$$

   $$= \left[\frac{12}{96} \times 818 \right] - 96$$

   $$= 102.25 - 96$$

   $$= 6.25$$

5. Calculate the degrees of freedom: the number of conditions minus one.

   $df = C - 1$

   $= 3 - 1$

   $= 2$

Notes on calculations in Box E

1 The Friedman test (related) is a non-parametric test based on ordinal data, in which three scores are ranked horizontally.
2 The test statistic is denoted by χ_r^2, which is pronounced 'ky r squared'. χ is the Greek letter 'chi'.
3 The calculations involve calculating the squares of the three rank totals and summing them to produce a sum of squares.
4 The formula in step 4 has to take into account the number of conditions and the squared rank totals.
5 You are told to calculate the degrees of freedom (*df*). The *df* are the number of conditions, *C*, minus 1 (in our example $3 - 1 = 2$). Note that you only need the *df* for experiments when there are relatively large numbers of participants doing all three conditions.

Looking up the significance of χ_r^2 in Table D or E

Note that there are quite often special tables for small numbers of conditions and participants and other tables for larger numbers.

Table D: up to nine participants

Table D covers three conditions for up to nine participants doing three conditions. Another point to notice about Table D is that it gives a list of all possible probabilities that can be read off for any calculated χ_r^2. The only relevant percentage values in Table D are those which achieve conventional levels of significance ($p < 0.05$). These are found at the bottom of the lists of probabilities.

The calculated χ_r^2 has to be equal to or larger than the values in the table. Our calculated χ_r^2 in Box E is 6.25 and there were 8 participants. Look down the column for $N = 8$ in Table D. For the calculated 6.25 the probability is 0.047. This probability is less than $p < 0.05$ so the null hypothesis can be rejected ($p < 0.05$).

Table E: more than nine participants

If there are more than nine participants it is possible to consult a more general statistical table, known as chi-square (χ^2) in Table E. To look up probabilities in Table E the *df* is the number of conditions, *C*, minus 1. In our example the *df* are $3 - 1 = 2$. In Table E look along the $df = 2$ row. The calculated 6.25 is larger than the value of 5.99 for $p < 0.05$. The null hypothesis can be rejected ($p < 0.05$).

Conclusions

It is essential to look at the means in Table 11.5 to check which of the illustrations was preferred by the children. It appears from the means in Table 11.5 that they preferred illustration B, since this received the highest ratings, with illustration C next and illustration A last. The Friedman test (related) can only test whether there are overall differences between conditions, which is the equivalent of a two-tailed hypothesis.

Progress box eleven

- In related designs three related scores in three conditions are produced by the same participants.
- The three related scores for each participant are ranked horizontally.
- The totals of ranks are added for each condition.
- The appropriate non-parametric statistical test for analysing related ordinal data for three conditions is the Friedman test (related).

? Question 11.3 Five participants were given three passages of prose to read, one typed in black print, one in red print and one in green print. Scores were the number of ideas recalled, as shown in Table 11.6.

(a) Using the data in Table 11.6, calculate the mean scores for the three conditions.

(b) What is the independent variable and what is the dependent variable?

(c) What is the appropriate statistical test and why?

(d) Following the step-by-step instructions 1 and 2 in Box E, assign horizontal ranks to the three scores for each participant.

(e) Add the rank totals for each condition.

Table 11.6 Data for Friedman test (related)

Participants	Condition 1 (black print)	Condition 2 (red print)	Condition 3 (green print)
1	4	5	6
2	2	7	7
3	6	6	8
4	3	7	5
5	3	8	9

12 Kruskal–Wallis test (unrelated)

12.1 Scores from different participants for three conditions

The Kruskal–Wallis test is a non-parametric test based on ranking ordinal data. As with the statistical tests for two conditions, we are introducing first the simpler non-parametric tests for dealing with three conditions.

In unrelated designs different participants do each condition. Because different participants do only one of the conditions, it is not possible to compare scores in three conditions for each participant. Instead all the individual scores have to be given overall rankings across all three conditions

An example is given in Table 12.1 for an experiment in which different groups of participants are presented with one each of three conditions. These conditions are very rare words (Group 1 doing Condition 1), fairly common words (Group 2 doing Condition 2) and very common words (Group 3 doing Condition 3).

Table 12.1 Recall scores for different types of word lists

Condition 1 Group 1 (rare words)		Condition 2 Group 2 (common words)		Condition 3 Group 3 (very common words)	
Scores	Ranks	Scores	Ranks	Scores	Ranks
2		3		11	
3		5		7	
1		6		4	
0		6		8	

12.2   Overall ranking of scores

You should remember from Chapter 7, which described the Mann–Whitney test (unrelated), that when there is no basis for direct comparisons, all the individual scores are ranked overall across all three conditions.

Exactly the same thing happens with the Kruskal–Wallis test (unrelated). The individual scores in all three conditions are assigned overall ranks.

In Table 12.2 overall ranks have been assigned to the individual scores in all three condition in the Ranks columns.

We will now take you through the assignment of overall ranks of all the scores across all three conditions, just as was done for two unrelated conditions for the Mann–Whitney (unrelated).

One participant in Condition 1 scored none of the very rare words correctly, which is a score of 0. This is the lowest score so it is assigned the lowest rank of 1. The next lowest score of 1 is also in Condition 1 and is ranked 2. Next comes a score of 2 also by a Condition 1 participant, which is ranked 3. The two next lowest scores of 3 by one participant in Condition 1 and also by one participant in Condition 2 are both assigned the average of the next available ranks of 4 and 5 giving tied ranks of 4.5. This procedure of assigning ranks is continued until all the scores have been assigned overall rankings, regardless of which condition they come from. For instance, a score of 4 by a participant in Condition 3 is ranked 6 while a higher score of 5 in Condition 2 is ranked 7. The top score of 11 by a participant in Condition 3 is assigned the highest rank of 12 (note that there are 12 participants, 4 in each group).

Table 12.2   Overall ranks of recall scores across conditions

Condition 1 Group 1		Condition 2 Group 2		Condition 3 Group 3	
Scores	*Ranks*	*Scores*	*Ranks*	*Scores*	*Ranks*
2	3	3	4.5	11	12
3	4.5	5	7	7	10
1	2	6	8.5	4	6
0	1	6	8.5	8	11

12.3   Totals of ranks for each condition

In order to decide whether the ranks are higher in one of the three conditions, the totals of ranks are added up separately for each condition. The aim is to check whether there are higher ranks in some conditions than other conditions.

There are two stages in assessing scores from different participants. The first stage is to carry out an overall ranking of all individual scores, regardless of which condition they are in. The second stage is to add the totals for each of the three conditions separately. The totals of the ranks for the three conditions are shown in Table 12.3.

Table 12.3   Totals of ranks for three conditions

	Condition 1 Group 1 (rare words)		Condition 2 Group 2 (common words)		Condition 3 Group 3 (very common words)	
	Scores	Ranks	Scores	Ranks	Scores	Ranks
	2	3	3	4.5	11	12
	3	4.5	5	7	7	10
	1	2	6	8.5	4	6
	0	1	6	8.5	8	11
Totals	6	10.5	20	28.5	30	39

? Question 12.1 (a) Would the rank totals in Table 12.3 support the hypothesis that groups of participants will recall more very common words (Condition 3) than rare words (Condition 1)?

(b) Calculate the means of the scores for each condition. Do these means reflect the same predicted differences between conditions?

The Kruskal–Wallis test (unrelated) can deal with three or more conditions. If there were four conditions the scores for the four conditions would have to be assigned overall ranks for all scores, regardless of the four conditions. The rank totals would then be added separately for each of the four conditions.

12.4 Selecting a statistical test in the Decision Chart

Differences between conditions?
The answer to this question is 'Yes' because the aim of the experiment is to test predicted differences between experimental conditions.

One or two variables?
Follow the line for one variable.

How many experimental conditions?
The answer is three or more conditions because the experiment is testing differences between three (or more) conditions..

Related or unrelated design?
The answer is unrelated design because different participants are doing each condition.

Non-parametric or parametric test?
The answer is non-parametric because non-parametric statistical tests are suitable for analysing ranked ordinal data.

You will find that if you answered the above four questions in the Decision Chart (inside back cover) as suggested, you will arrive at the Kruskal–Wallis test (unrelated). The Kruskal–Wallis (unrelated) is the appropriate non-parametric test for an unrelated design with three or more conditions.

12.5 Using the Kruskal–Wallis test (unrelated)

When to use

The Kruskal–Wallis test (unrelated) should be used for an unrelated design when different participants are doing three (or more) conditions and the data are ordinal.

Research hypothesis

The prediction was that the number of illustrations in a text would affect participants' recalls of ideas from the text.

Sample data

Three groups of different participants were presented with texts to read. The first group read texts which were highly illustrated (Condition 1), the second group read tests with some illustrations (Condition 2), the third group read tests with no illustrations (Condition 3). The dependent variable was the number of ideas recalled from each text. The scores for each group of different participants is shown in Table 12.4.

Table 12.4   Number of ideas recalled for illustrated texts

	Condition 1 (highly illustrated text)		Condition 2 (text with some illustrations)		Condition 3 (text with no illustrations)	
	Scores	Ranks	Scores	Ranks	Scores	Ranks
	19	10	14	6	12	3.5
	21	11	15	7	12	3.5
	17	9	9	1	13	5
	16	8			10	2
Rank totals		38		14		14
Means	18.25		12.67		11.75	

Notes on Table 12.4
1 Check the overall ranks assigned to the individual scores across all three conditions.
2 The rank totals are added for each of the three conditions.
3 Note that in Table 12.4 there are unequal numbers of participants in the three conditions (4 in Condition 1, 3 in Condition 2 and 4 in Condition 3). These unequal numbers of participants for the three conditions will affect how probabilities are looked up in the statistical tables.

Rationale

The aim of the Kruskal–Wallis test (unrelated) is to test whether the rank totals are different for three groups of participants in three conditions. If there are random differences between the rank totals for all three conditions, as stated by the null hypothesis, we would expect the rank totals to be approximately equal, because there would be equal numbers of low and high ranks in each of the conditions. If the rank totals show a preponderance of high or low ranks in one or other of the conditions, the null hypothesis can be rejected.

Step-by-step instructions for performing the Kruskal–Wallis test (unrelated)

These are given in Box F.

■ **Box F**

Step-by-step instructions for calculating the value of H

1   Rank *all* the scores *across* conditions as an *overall* set of ranks, giving 1 to the smallest score and so on.

    See the 'Ranks' columns in Table 12.4 which contain the overall ranks of all scores taken together

2   Calculate rank totals for each condition.

    $T_1 = 38, T_2 = 14, T_3 = 14$

3   Note the following symbols:

    N = total number of participants

    $N = 11$

    n = number of participants in each group

    $n_1 = 4, n_2 = 3, n_3 = 4$

    T^2 = squares of the rank totals for each condition

    $T_1^2 = 38^2, T_2^2 = 14^2, T_3^2 = 14^2$

    $\dfrac{\Sigma T^2}{n}$ = sum of the squared rank totals for each condition divided by the number of subjects in that condition

4   Calculate the value of H using the formula

$$H = \left[\frac{12}{N(N+1)} \Sigma \frac{T^2}{n}\right] - 3(N+1)$$

$$H = \left[\frac{12}{11 \times 12}\left(\frac{38^2}{4} + \frac{14^2}{3} + \frac{14^2}{4}\right)\right]$$
$$-3 \times 12$$

$$= \left[\frac{12}{132}\left(\frac{1444}{4} + \frac{196}{3} + \frac{196}{4}\right)\right] - 36$$

$$= 0.091(361 + 65.33 + 49) - 36$$

$$= 43.2 - 36$$

$$= 7.2$$

5   Calculate the degrees of freedom: the number of conditions (C) minus one.

$$df = C - 1$$
$$= 3 - 1$$
$$= 2$$

Notes on calculations in Box F

1 The Kruskal–Wallis test (unrelated) is a non-parametric test based on ordinal data, in which overall scores are ranked and rank totals calculated.
2 The calculations involve calculating the squares of the rank totals and summing them to produce a sum of squares.
3 The formula in step 4 for calculating H has to take into account the number of conditions and the number of participants in each group.
4 You are told to calculate degrees of freedom (df). The df are the number of conditions (C) minus 1 (in our example $3 - 1 = 2$). Note that you only need the df for experiments with relatively large numbers of participants in each group.

Looking up the significance of H in Tables F and E

Note that there are quite often special tables for small numbers of conditions and participants and other tables for larger numbers.

Table F: up to five participants

Table F covers three conditions, with different numbers of participants in each group, up to 5 participants in each group.

In Table F you have to look up the size of the groups in an experiment. In our example the sizes of groups are $n_1 = 4$, $n_2 = 3$, $n_3 = 4$. When you look up the group sizes in Table F it does not matter about the order of the group sizes. The appropriate sizes are 4, 4, 3.

The calculated H has to be equal to or larger than the values in the tables. The first column for each set of group sizes gives the values of H. The final column gives the probabilities (p) associated with each value of H. In our example the calculated H in Box F is 7.2. Look at the probabilities for H for the 4, 4, 3 group sizes. There is an H of 7.1364, which is the nearest to 7.2. The probability for this value of H is $p < 0.01$. The null hypothesis can be rejected ($p < 0.01$)

Table E: more than five participants

In most experiments there will be more than five participants in each group. If you have more than three conditions and/or more than 5 participants per group, you will have to consult a more general statistical Table E known as 'chi-square'. To look up probabilities in Table E the df is the number of conditions, C, minus 1. In our example $df = 3 - 1 = 2$. In Table E look along the $df = 2$ row. The calculated H of 7.2 is larger than the value of 5.99 for $p < 0.05$. The null hypothesis can be rejected ($p < 0.05$).

Conclusions

It is essential to look up the means in Table 12.4 to check which texts with illustrations resulted in more ideas being recalled. The means show that more ideas were recalled from the highly illustrated texts in Condition 1 than from either of the other two texts. The Kruskal–Wallis test (unrelated) can only test whether there are overall differences between conditions, which is the equivalent of a two-tailed hypothesis.

12.6 Note about names of non-parametric tests

Sometimes students find it quite difficult to remember the names of non-parametric tests. A tip about names for related and unrelated tests is as follows, which is just a coincidence!

Related tests have just one name: Wilcoxon (related) for two conditions; Friedman (related) for three conditions.

Unrelated tests were invented by two researchers so are named after both: Mann–Whitney (unrelated) for two conditions; Kruskal–Wallis (unrelated) for three conditions.

 Progress box twelve

- In unrelated designs the scores in all three conditions are produced by different participants.
- Individual scores are assigned overall ranks across all conditions.
- The totals of ranks are added separately for each condition.
- The appropriate non-parametric statistical test for analysing unrelated ordinal data for three conditions is the Kruskal–Wallis test (unrelated).

Part III Analysis of variance

13 Introduction to ANOVA

13.1 Parametric tests

All the tests described in Part III are parametric tests. You will find that some of the concepts of analysing variance seem quite familiar.

The t tests, which were described in Chapters 8, 9 and 10, are also parametric tests. Outlined below are some of the concepts that apply to all parametric tests:

Numerical calculations on interval data. All parametric tests are based on carrying out numerical calculations on interval data.

Ratios of variances. Parametric tests calculate ratios between predicted variance and total variance.

Calculating variances. It is a general principle that variance is calculated by squaring numbers and summing the squares in various combinations. You will be given detailed information about which sums of squares to calculate in the step-by-step instructions for each type of ANOVA.

13.2 Analysis of variance

The letters ANOVA stand for ANalysis Of VAriance. Analysing variance is a basic feature of all parametric tests. One of the special advantages of ANOVA is that total variance can be subdivided into other types of variance. Total variance includes both predicted variance and variance due to irrelevant variables. With ANOVA, rather than comparing predicted variance against total variance, it is possible to subdivide total variance into other kinds of variance.

Two subdivisions of total variance are: predicted variance; and error variance due to unpredicted irrelevant variables.

Predicted variance is called *between-conditions* variance. This is because the researcher has predicted differences between conditions as a result of the selected independent variable.

Variance due to unpredicted variables is called *error variance*. The reason for this term is that, from the point of view of the experimenter, anything that has not been predicted represents error.

Experimenters naturally try to reduce unpredicted error. One example of unpredicted error might be if the same participants do all the experimental conditions in the same order, leading to possible bias in participants' responses. A researcher routinely counterbalances the order of conditions so as to remove order effects from possible error variance.

To summarize the argument so far, there are three different kinds of variance in ANOVA. These are:

Predicted variance
Error variance
Total variance

It is important to note that predicted variance and error variance together add up to total variance.

13.3   Sources of variance

Different kinds of variance are very commonly expressed as *sources* of variance. This term is used to indicate that each kind of variance is caused by a different type of variable. These variables are the sources of the variance. The sources of variance in ANOVA are shown in Table 13.1.

In ANOVA the predicted between-conditions variance is calculated on the basis of predicted differences in scores between conditions.

Total variance is calculated on the basis of differences in individual scores produced by all participants in the experiment.

Error variance is calculated by subtracting predicted variance from total variance. The rationale for this is that error variance is everything that is left over after predicted variance has been accounted for.

Table 13.1   ANOVA sources of variance

Sources of variance	*Types of variance*
Independent variables (predicted)	Between-conditions variance
Irrelevant variables (unpredicted)	Error variance
Combination of independent variables and irrelevant variables	Total variance

In ANOVA, tests of significance are based on the ratio of predicted, between-conditions variance to error variance.

13.4 Degrees of freedom

There is one other important consideration that has to be taken into account when calculating variances and when looking up statistics in parametric statistics tables. This is the need to identify degrees of freedom (*df*).

You have been instructed to calculate *df* in some of the step-by-step instructions for earlier tests. The rationale for degrees of freedom arises from the notion that parametric tests calculate variances based on variability in scores. It is essential that all scores are 'free' to vary. The issue is whether all scores from an experiment are equally variable.

The concept of degrees of freedom is quite a difficult one to grasp. An experimental example might help.

Suppose you carry out an experiment and calculate the total of the scores. When copying out the scores later, you forget to include one of the scores from one of the six participants. You end up with the scores shown in Table 13.2.

You do not need to panic because you know that, given five scores and the total of all six scores, you can calculate the forgotten score for participant 6. All you have to do is to subtract the five scores from the total of 75; the score for participant 6 could only have been 15. The implication is that the score for that participant is predictable from knowing the other scores and the total. So it has no 'freedom' to vary.

Degrees of freedom take into account the fact that one of the scores does not vary because it can be predicted from the other five scores. 'Degrees of freedom' is a term to indicate that all the other scores can vary.

Table 13.2 Scores used for calculating degrees of freedom

Participant	Score
1	12
2	13
3	10
4	11
5	14
6	–
Total	75

Degrees of freedom are calculated as the total number of scores (N) minus one score ($N - 1$). In Table 13.2 there are six scores but only five scores can vary. Subtracting 1 from 6 gives $df = N - 1 = 5$. This confirms that only five scores are free to vary.

Subtracting 1 is a very general principle for calculating df. You will find that df are required for calculating ratios of variance. You will also find that df are important when looking up ratios in ANOVA statistical tables.

This is a very brief introduction to calculating degrees of freedom. Sometimes df for combinations of variances have to be added or multiplied to obtain total df. In the step-by-step instruction for each type of ANOVA you will be given detailed instructions about the calculation of df.

? Question 13.1 In Table 13.3 there are four scores with one missing score and a total of 56.

(a) Calculate score 4.

(b) What are the degrees of freedom?

Table 13.3 Calculating missing scores

Score 1	8
Score 2	12
Score 3	20
Score 4	–
Total score	56

13.5 Requirements for parametric tests

There are three main requirements for parametric tests. These apply to ANOVA and also to parametric t tests. These include (a) the measurement of data, (b) the way in which the total scores are distributed and (c) whether the scores are distributed equally in the experimental conditions.

We can deal quite easily with measurement of data. Because ANOVA and t tests are parametric statistical tests, which involve numerical calculations based on sums of squares, the first requirement is that that data must be interval data, with equal intervals between scores on a continuous numerical scale.

The question of the distribution of scores is more complex and we will describe these concepts in the next section.

13.6   Normal distribution

A second requirement for parametric tests is that scores should be normally distributed.

The essence of a normal distribution of scores is that there tend to be more middle-range scores than extreme scores. This is a very general characteristic of distributions of scores. Think about the heights of the adult population. You would expect to find more people in the middle range of heights (say 4.5–6 ft) than adults who are extremely tall (6–7 ft) or extremely short (3–4 ft).

A normal distribution will be symmetrical, with equal numbers of extreme scores at each end. Staying with the height example, the requirement is that there should be approximately equal numbers of rather short people and very tall people.

One way to demonstrate this is to draw a histogram of all the scores in an experiment, as shown in Figure 13.1. The possible scores are listed along the bottom line. For every participant who scores a particular score a box is added. The height of the boxes for each score represents the number of participants who had that particular score. For example, six participants had a score of 5.

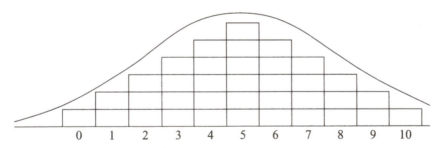

Figure 13.1   Normal distribution

? Question 13.2   (a) How many participants had a score of 1?

(b) How many participants had a score of 6?

What the curved line in Figure 13.1 shows is a theoretical normal distribution for an unlimited number of scores.

A third formal requirement for parametric data is termed homogeneity of variance. The word 'homogeneity' means 'sameness'. This implies that the variability of the scores in each condition should be approximately the same.

The idea is that it would be difficult to make a comparison between conditions based on very different distributions of scores. An example would be if the scores in one condition were bunched around scores of 10, 11 and 12, compared with the scores in another condition ranging from 100 down to 1. Fortunately, such wide differences in variance between two conditions are a rare occurrence.

It has been shown that, as long as there are equal numbers of participants in each condition, the results of parametric tests are fairly robust. The word 'robust' implies that, given that the data are approximately normally distributed and there are not too wide discrepancies in condition variances, the results of parametric tests will give a reasonably accurate analysis of the data from an experiment. This is a good reason for always allocating the same number of participants to each experimental condition.

A rough check of whether scores from an experiment are approximately normal is to draw a histogram of all the scores. You could draw histograms for the scores in each condition to see whether distributions in each condition are approximately equal. There are also more precise ways of ways of checking a normal distribution and homogeneity of variance using statistical software.

13.7   Computer statistical packages

Many students will have access to a commonly used computer statistical package called SPSS. This statistical software is likely to be available in psychology departments. It is also possible to download SPSS from the Internet.

There are several advantages to using the SPSS computer package. It carries out all the calculations needed to produce ratios of variance and will even look up the statistical tables to provide a significance level.

The SPSS package also automatically checks whether the data from an experiment are approximately normally distributed and whether the scores in each condition reach an acceptable homogeneity of variance.

Pressing a button on a computer to carry out all statistical calculations and to deliver significance levels may seem wonderful. However, note the following words of warning:

1 You may not understand the rationale for selecting an appropriate statistical test.

2 You may forget how to look up statistical tables for levels of significance.
3 Sometimes students calculate a level of significance and do not check the means to decide whether the significant results support the predictions in the right direction as predicted by the original research hypothesis.

Despite all the advantages of SPSS, we will still be presenting boxes with step-by-step instructions for calculating ANOVA. There are several reasons for this decision. The first reason is that you may not have access to the SPSS computer program. An even more important reason is that it is useful to get some idea of how sums of squares contribute to ratios of variances.

ANOVA (unrelated) is the easiest to calculate so we will be presenting this type of ANOVA first. We will take you through the calculations at every stage. This will help you to understand how the various formulae are unpacked.

For later, more complex types of ANOVA, we will give the formulae and the degrees of freedom necessary for calculating ratios and looking them up in ANOVA statistical tables. You will be able to refer to the full calculations in the ANOVA (unrelated) box if you need to calculate any of the same sums of squares using a calculator or a computer package.

 Progress box thirteen

- The letters ANOVA stand for 'analysis of variance'.
- ANOVA analyses three sources of variance: between-conditions variance (predicted independent variable); error variance (unpredicted irrelevant variables); and total variance (all the variance in scores).
- Ratios are calculated between predicted variance and error variance by calculating sums of squares.
- Degrees of freedom are calculated by deducting one predictable score $(N-1)$.
- The main requirements for ANOVA parametric tests are that the data are interval, the scores are normally distributed and that the variances in conditions are approximately the same.
- The SPSS computer program can be used to do calculations and to check the requirements for parametric tests. But it is important to understand the rationale for statistical tests.

14 One-way ANOVA (unrelated)

14.1 Scores from different participants

One-way ANOVA tests three (or more) conditions. In ANOVA (unrelated) different groups of participants do each condition. Because different participants do only one of the experimental conditions, it is not possible to compare related scores for all conditions for each participant. Instead the individual scores have to be treated as independent scores from different participants.

The term 'one-way ANOVA' indicates that there is only one independent variable to be tested. This contrasts with later accounts of two-way ANOVA, which is designed for two variables.

14.2 Definitions of variance

For ANOVA (unrelated) three sources of variance can be calculated. These include:

Between-conditions variance (predicted)
Error variance (due to irrelevant variables and including individual differences between participants)
Total variance (combined between conditions and error variance).

14.3 Selecting a statistical test in the Decision Chart

Differences between conditions?
The answer to this question is 'Yes' because the aim of the experiment is to test predicted differences between experimental conditions.

One or two variables?
The answer for one-way ANOVA is one variable.

How many experimental conditions?
The answer is three or more conditions because the experiment is testing differences between three (or more) conditions.

Related or unrelated design?
The answer is unrelated design because different participants are doing each condition.

Non-parametric or parametric test?
The answer is parametric because parametric statistical tests are suitable for analysing numerical interval data.

You will find that if you answered the above five questions in the Decision Chart (inside back cover) as suggested, you will arrive at one-way ANOVA (unrelated). ANOVA (unrelated) is the appropriate parametric test for a one-way unrelated design with three (or more) conditions.

14.4   Using one-way ANOVA (unrelated)

When to use

One-way ANOVA (unrelated) should be used for an unrelated design when different participants are doing three (or more) conditions testing one independent variable and the data are interval.

Research hypothesis

The experimenter predicted that three presentation rates of lists of words would have an effect on recall scores.

Sample data

Three different groups of six subjects were presented with lists of ten words to learn. Group 1 was presented with words at a slow rate of presentation of one word every 5 seconds (Condition 1), Group 2 with a medium presentation rate of one word every 2 seconds (Condition 2) and Group 3 with a fast presentation rate of one word every second (Condition 3). The recall scores are shown in Table 14.1.

Table 14.1   Number of words recalled for three presentation rates

	Condition 1 (slow rate)	Condition 2 (medium rate)	Condition 3 (fast rate)	
	8	7	4	
	7	8	5	
	9	5	3	
	5	4	6	
	6	6	2	
	8	7	4	
Totals (*T*)	43	37	24	104 Grand total
Means	7.17	6.17	4	

Notes on Table 14.1
1 The means have been calculated for each of the conditions.
2 The totals for the six participants in each condition have been calculated.
3 The grand total (104) of the 18 scores in all three conditions has also been calculated.

Rationale

The aim of ANOVA is to compare ratios of variances. The independent variable of three presentation rates represents the predicted differences between the three conditions (between-conditions variance). Differences in scores due to irrelevant variables represent error variance.

The prediction is that the variance between conditions will be relatively large compared with the error variance due to irrelevant variables. If there are random differences between conditions, as stated by the null hypothesis, the variance due to the predicted differences between conditions will be small in relation to error variance. In this case, the null hypothesis cannot be rejected.

Step-by-step instructions for calculating ANOVA (unrelated)

These are given in Box G.

Box G

Step-by-step instructions for calculating one-way *F* ratios (unrelated)

1 Note the following symbols (see Table 14.1):

$\sum T^2$ = sum of squared totals for each condition $\qquad \sum T^2 = 43^2 + 37^2 + 24^2$

n = number of participants in each condition $\qquad n = 6$

N = total number of scores $\qquad N = 18$

$(\sum x)^2$ = grand total squared $\qquad (\sum x)^2 = 104^2$

$\dfrac{(\sum x)^2}{N}$ = constant to be subtracted from all sums of squares $\qquad \dfrac{104^2}{18} = \dfrac{10{,}816}{18} = 600.89$

$\sum x^2$ = sum of each individual score squared

2 Calculate SS_{bet}

$$\frac{\sum T^2}{n} - \frac{(\sum x)^2}{N}$$

$$= \frac{43^2 + 37^2 + 24^2}{6} - 600.89$$
$$= 632.33 - 600.89$$
$$= 31.44$$

3 Calculate SS_{tot}

$$\sum x^2 - \frac{(\sum x)^2}{N}$$

$$= 8^2 + 7^2 + 9^2 + 5^2 + 6^2 + 8^2$$
$$+ 7^2 + 8^2 + 5^2 + 4^2 + 6^2 + 7^2$$
$$+ 4^2 + 5^2 + 3^2 + 6^2 + 2^2 + 4^2$$
$$- 600.89$$
$$= 664 - 600.89$$
$$= 63.11$$

4 Calculate SS_{error}

$$SS_{tot} - SS_{bet}$$

$$= 63.11 - 31.44$$
$$= 31.67$$

5 Calculate the degrees of freedom

df_{bet} = number of conditions − 1 $\qquad df_{bet} = 3 - 1 = 2$
$df_{tot} = N - 1$ $\qquad df_{tot} = 18 - 1 = 17$
$df_{error} = df_{tot} - df_{bet}$ $\qquad df_{error} = 17 - 2 = 15$

6 Divide each SS by df to obtain MS

$$MS_{bet} = \frac{SS_{bet}}{df_{bet}}$$

$$= \frac{31.44}{2} = 15.72$$

$$MS_{error} = \frac{SS_{error}}{df_{error}}$$

$$= \frac{31.67}{15} = 2.11$$

7   Calculate the F ratio for MS_{bet} over MS_{error}
     allocating the correct df to MS_{bet} and MS_{error}

   F ratio for $MS_{bet} = \dfrac{MS_{bet}}{MS_{error}}$ $F_{2,15} = \dfrac{15.72}{2.11} = 7.45$

8   The completed ANOVA table is shown in
     Table 14.2.

Notes on calculations in Box G

1 Note the definitions of the symbols and the calculation of a constant,
   which will be subtracted from all sums of squares. This is the grand total
   of all scores squared and divided by N.

2 Between-conditions variance (SS_{bet}) is calculated by summing the
   squared totals for each condition, dividing the sum by n (participants
   in each condition) and subtracting the constant.

3 Total variance (SS_{tot}) is calculated by summing the squares of all the
   scores and subtracting the constant.

4 Error variance (SS_{error}) is calculated by subtracting predicted variance
   (SS_{bet}) from total variance (SS_{tot}).

5 Rules are given for calculating the degrees of freedom (df) by subtracting 1 for each type of variance.

6 MS_{bet} and MS_{error} are calculated by dividing the sums of squares (SS)
   by the df.

7 The F ratio is calculated by dividing MS_{bet} by MS_{error}. Note that df
   are given for F ($df_{bet} = 2$, $df_{error} = 15$).

Table 14.2   One-way ANOVA table (unrelated)

Sources of variance	*Sums of squares*	*Degrees of freedom*	*Mean squares*	*F ratio*
Presentation rate	31.44	2	15.72	$F_{2,15} = 7.45$
Error	31.67	15	2.11	
Total	63.11	17		

Looking up the significance of *F* in Table G

Tables G(1) and G(2) are the appropriate tables for all ANOVA tests.
Table G(1) gives the values for $p < 0.05$. Table G(2) gives the values for $p <$
0.01. The calculated F has to be equal to or larger than these values. You
need to use the degrees of freedom for the between-conditions variance

and the error variance (see step 5 in Box G). (In our example these are $df_{bet} = 2$, $df_{error} = 15$.)

In Table G(1) df_{bet} is shown along the v_1 row and df_{error} is shown down the v_2 column. Locate 2 on v_1 along the top line and follow the v_2 column down until you find 15. Where they intersect is the critical value. In Table G(1) the value for $F_{2,15}$ is 3.68 for $p < 0.05$. The calculated F of 7.45 in Box G is larger than 3.68, so the null hypothesis can be rejected ($p < 0.05$). The next step is to see whether the calculated value of F of 7.45 is larger than the critical value of 6.36 in Table G (2) for $df = 2, 15$ ($p < 0.01$). The calculated F is larger than the value of 6.36 so the null hypothesis can be rejected ($p < 0.01$).

Conclusions

It is essential to look back at Table 14.1 to check the differences between the means in the three conditions. There are differences between the means for the three conditions with different presentation rates. This result supports the research hypothesis that presentation rates of words lists would have an effect on recall scores, with the fewest words recalled for the fast presentation rate in Condition 3.

Note that ANOVA only tells you whether there are overall significant differences between the experimental conditions, which is equivalent to a two-tailed hypothesis. In Chapter 16 tests for identifying the effects of individual conditions will be discussed.

 Progress box fourteen

- In one-way ANOVA there is one independent variable.
- In ANOVA (unrelated) the scores are produced by different participants.
- Three sources of variance are tested by ANOVA (unrelated): between-conditions variance, error variance and total variance.
- The appropriate parametric test for analysing three sources of variance in an unrelated design is one-way ANOVA (unrelated).

15 One-way ANOVA (related)

15.1 Scores from same participants

One-way ANOVA tests three (or more) conditions. In ANOVA (related) the same participants do all the conditions. Each participant produces three scores, one in each of three conditions. This makes it possible to make a direct comparison between each participant's three scores in all the conditions.

The term 'one-way ANOVA' indicates that there is only one independent variable to be tested. This contrasts with later accounts of two-way ANOVA, which is designed for two variables.

15.2 Definitions of variance

Because there are three related scores for each participant, it is possible to calculate the variance between the three related scores for each participant. Each participant will have a different set of three related scores. These differences between participants provide the basis for calculating the variance due to individual differences between participants.

In ANOVA (related) it is possible to identify an extra type of variance, which represents individual variance between participants. One important result of being able to calculate individual variance between participants is that for ANOVA (related) four kinds of variance can be calculated. These include:

Between-conditions variance (predicted)
Individual variance (based on differences between related scores by each participant)
Error variance (due to irrelevant variables)
Total variance (including all the above kinds of variances).

The net result of four types of variance is that the error variance has been split into two. You will remember from Section 14.2 that error variance was due to all irrelevant variables including individual differences between participants. This was because in ANOVA (unrelated) there was no basis for comparing related scores.

With ANOVA (related) the individual variance between participants can be calculated as a separate source of variance. It is for this reason that error variance no longer includes individual differences between participants.

15.3   Selecting a statistical test in the Decision Chart

Differences between conditions?
The answer to this question is 'Yes' because the aim of the experiment is to test predicted differences between experimental conditions.

One or two variables?
The answer for one-way ANOVA is one variable.

How many experimental conditions?
The answer is three or more conditions because the experiment is testing differences between three (or more) conditions.

Related or unrelated design?
The answer is related design because the same participants are doing all conditions.

Non-parametric or parametric test?
The answer is parametric because parametric statistical tests are suitable for analysing numerical interval data.

You will find that if you answered the above five questions in the Decision Chart as suggested, you will arrive at one-way ANOVA (related). ANOVA (related) is the appropriate parametric test for a one-way related design with three (or more) conditions.

15.4   Using one-way ANOVA (related)

When to use

One-way ANOVA (related) should be used when the same participants are doing three (or more) conditions testing one independent variable and the data are interval.

Research hypothesis

The experimenter predicted that three presentation rates of lists of words would have an effect on recall scores.

Sample data

The same six participants were presented with Condition 1 (words at a slow rate of presentation of one word every 5 seconds), Condition 2 (words at a medium rate of one word every 2 seconds) and Condition 3 (words at a fast rate of one word every second). The recall scores for the three conditions are shown in Table 15.1.

? Question 15.1 What precautions should be taken by an experimenter to offset the possible order effects of participants doing all three conditions in the same order?

Table 15.1   Number of words recalled for three presentation rates

Participants	Condition 1 (slow rate)	Condition 2 (medium rate)	Condition 3 (fast rate)	Totals for participants (T_s)
1	8	7	4	19
2	7	8	5	20
3	9	5	3	17
4	5	4	6	15
5	6	6	2	14
6	8	7	4	19
Totals (T)	43	37	24	104 Grand total
Means	7.17	6.17	4	

Notes on Table 15.1
1 The scores and totals in Table 15.1 are the same as in Table 14.1 in Chapter 14.
2 Because all participants are doing all conditions the participants are listed in the first column. This makes it clear that each participant produces three related scores, one in each condition.
3 The main difference with ANOVA (unrelated) is that the totals of related scores have been calculated for each of the six participants. These totals appear in the last column of Table 15.1.

Rationale

The aim of ANOVA is to compare ratios of variances. The independent variable of three presentation rates represents the predicted differences between the three conditions (between-conditions variance). Differences in scores due to irrelevant variables represent error variance. Differences between participants represent individual variance.

The prediction is that the variance between conditions will be relatively large compared with the error variance due to irrelevant variables. If there are random differences between conditions, as stated by the null hypothesis, the variance due to the predicted differences between conditions will be small in relation to error variance. In this case, the null hypothesis cannot be rejected. It is normal to compare individual variance with error variance. But the experimenter will be pleased if there are no significant differences between individual participants.

Step-by-step instructions for calculating ANOVA (related)

These are given in Box H.

 Box H

Step-by-step instruction for calculating one-way *F* ratios (related)

1 Note the following symbols (see Table 15.1):

$\sum T^2$ = sum of squared total for each condition

$\sum T^2 = 43^2 + 37^2 + 24^2$

$\sum T_s^2$ = sum of squared totals for each participant

$\sum T_s^2 = 19^2 + 20^2 + 17^2 + 15^2 + 14^2 + 19^2$

n = number of participants

$n = 6$

c = number of conditions

$c = 3$

N = number of scores

$N = 18$

$(\sum x)^2$ = grand total squared

$(\sum x)^2 = 104^2$

$\dfrac{(\sum x)^2}{N}$ = constant to be subtracted from all SS

$\dfrac{104^2}{18} = \dfrac{10816}{18} = 600.89$

$\sum x^2$ = sum of each individual score squared

2   Calculate SS_{bet}

$$\frac{\Sigma T^2}{n} - \frac{(\Sigma x)^2}{N}$$

$$= \frac{43^2 + 37^2 + 24^2}{6} - 600.89$$

$$= 632.33 - 600.89$$

$$= 31.44$$

3   Calculate SS_{subj}

$$\frac{\Sigma T_s^2}{c} - \frac{(\Sigma x)^2}{N}$$

$$= \frac{19^2 + 20^2 + 17^2 + 15^2 + 14^2 + 19^2}{3}$$

$$- 600.89$$

$$= 610.67 - 600.89$$

$$= 9.78$$

4   Calculate SS_{tot}

$$\Sigma x^2 - \frac{(\Sigma x)^2}{N}$$

$$= 8^2 + 7^2 + 9^2 + 5^2 + 6^2 + 8^2 + 7^2 + 8^2 + 5^2$$
$$+ 4^2 + 6^2 + 7^2 + 4^2 + 5^2 + 3^2 + 6^2 + 2^2$$
$$+ 4^2 - 600.89$$

$$= 664 - 600.89$$

$$= 63.11$$

5   Calculate SS_{error}

$$SS_{tot} - SS_{bet} - SS_{subj}$$

$$= 63.11 - 31.44 - 9.78$$

$$= 21.89$$

6   Calculate the degrees of freedom

df_{bet} = number of conditions − 1 $df_{bet} = 3 - 1 = 2$

df_{subj} = number of subjects − 1 $df_{subj} = 6 - 1 = 5$

$df_{tot} = N - 1$ $df_{tot} = 18 - 1 = 17$

$df_{error} = df_{tot} - df_{bet} - df_{subj}$ $df_{error} = 17 - 2 - 5 = 10$

7   Divide each SS by df to obtain MS

$$MS_{bet} = \frac{SS_{bet}}{df_{bet}}$$

$$= \frac{31.44}{2} = 15.72$$

$$MS_{subj} = \frac{SS_{subj}}{df_{subj}}$$

$$= \frac{9.78}{5} = 1.956$$

$$MS_{error} = \frac{SS_{error}}{df_{error}}$$

$$= \frac{21.89}{10} = 2.189$$

8   Calculate F ratios for MS_{bet} over MS_{error} and for MS_{subj} over MS_{error} allocating the correct df to the F ratios:

$$F \text{ ratio for } MS_{bet} = \frac{MS_{bet}}{MS_{error}}$$

$$F_{2,10} = \frac{15.72}{2.189} = 7.18$$

$$F \text{ ratio for } MS_{subj} = \frac{MS_{subj}}{MS_{error}} \qquad\qquad F_{5,10} = \frac{1.956}{2.189} = 0.8935$$

9 The completed ANOVA is shown in Table 15.2.

Notes on calculations in Box H

1 Some of the calculations of sums of squares are exactly the same as in Box G in Chapter 14, as are the symbols in step 1, SS_{bet} in step 2 and SS_{tot} in step 4. But there are also new sources of variance for ANOVA (related).

2 In statistical tables it is universal to use the older notation SS_{subj} to refer to individual differences between participants (individual variance). You will find this notation used in all statistical textbooks (rather than participant variance). To calculate SS_{subj} the squared totals of T_s are summed and divided by the number of conditions, and the constant subtracted.

3 In step 5 all other variances are subtracted from SS_{total}. Note that subtracting SS_{subj} as well results in a smaller SS_{error}.

4 In step 6 the degrees of freedom are calculated for you. Because of the extra SS_{subj} the *df* are more complicated than for ANOVA (unrelated), but you should follow the instructions.

5 In step 7 MS_{bet}, MS_{subj} and MS_{error} are calculated by dividing the sums of squares (*SS*) by the *df*.

6 In step 8 *F* ratios are calculated for MS_{bet} and MS_{subj} over MS_{error}. Each *F* ratio indicates the relevant *df* (2,10 and 5,10).

Table 15.2 One-way ANOVA (related)

Sources of variance	Sums of squares	Degrees of freedom	Mean squares	F ratios
Presentation rate	31.44	2	15.72	$F_{2,10} = 7.18$
Participants (*SS*)	9.78	5	1.956	$F_{5,10} = 0.8935$
Error	21.89	10	2.189	
Total	63.11	17		

Looking up the significance of *F* in Table G

Tables G(1) and G(2) are the appropriate tables for all ANOVA tests. Table G(1) gives the values for $p < 0.05$. Table G(2) gives the values for $p < 0.01$.

The calculated F has to be equal to or larger than the values in the tables. You need to use the df for the between-conditions variance, the error variance and the individual variance (see step 6 in Box H). (In our example these are $df_{bet} = 2$, $df_{error} = 10$, $df_{subj} = 5$.)

In Table G(1) df_{bet} is shown along the v1 row on the top line and the df_{error} down the v2 column. Locate 2 on v1 along the top line and follow down the v2 column to find 10. Where they intersect is the critical value. In Table G(1) the value for $F_{2,10}$ is 4.10. The calculated F of 7.18 in Box H is larger than 4.10, so the null hypothesis can be rejected ($p < 0.05$). The next step is to see whether the calculated F of 7.18 is larger than the value in Table G(2) for df 2,10 ($p < 0.01$). 7.18 is smaller than the critical value of 7.56 so the null hypothesis cannot be rejected at this significance level.

It is common practice to test the significance of the F ratio for individual variance, hoping that individual differences between participants will not be a significant source of variance. In our example, the calculated F for SS_{subj} of 0.8935 (df 5,10) is smaller than the value of 3.33 in Table G (1) and so the differences between participants are not significant.

Conclusions

It is essential to look back at the means in Table 15.1 to check whether there are differences between the means for the three conditions. There are differences between the means for the three conditions with different presentation rates of words, which have been shown to be significant ($p < 0.05$). This supports the research hypothesis that presenting words at faster or slower presentation rates would have an effect on recall scores.

Note that ANOVA only tells you whether there are overall significant differences between experimental conditions, which is the equivalent of a two-tailed hypothesis. In Chapter 16 tests for identifying the effects of individual conditions will be discussed.

 Progress box fifteen

- In one-way ANOVA (related) there is one independent variable.
- In ANOVA (related) the scores are produced by the same participants.
- Four sources of variance are tested by ANOVA (related): between-conditions variance, individual variance, error variance and total variance.
- The appropriate parametric test for analysing four sources of variance in a related design is one-way ANOVA (related).

16 Comparisons between ANOVA conditions

16.1 Overall differences in ANOVA

In the conclusion sections in Chapters 14 and 15, we made the point that ANOVA only provides information about overall differences between experimental conditions. However clear the differences seem to be between the means for individual conditions, ANOVA tables can only test whether there are overall significant differences. ANOVA cannot identify which individual conditions contributed most to these overall differences.

What researchers would like to do is identify which individual conditions contribute to the significant overall differences in scores in the experimental conditions. In order to achieve this they need to identify patterns of the mean scores for all the conditions.

The first step is to look at the mean scores to see if some of them indicate that not all the experimental conditions have contributed to the overall ANOVA in exactly the same way.

16.2 Graphs showing patterns of mean scores

One method for displaying the pattern of mean scores is to draw them in the form of a graph. A graph of mean scores is shown in Figure 16.1. Every graph has a horizontal line and a vertical line; each of these is called an axis.

In the case of Figure 16.1 the three mean scores are for three rates of presenting lists of words: A (fast), B (medium) and C (slow). The three presentation rates are listed along the horizontal axis and recall scores are listed up the vertical axis. For each presentation rate the mean score is marked.

Looking at these mean scores it is obvious that, rather than the three conditions contributing equally to the one-way ANOVA, there is a definite

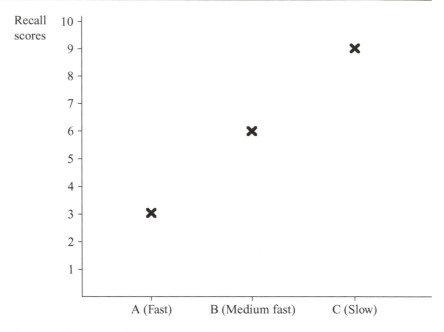

Figure 16.1   Graph showing recall scores for three presentation rates

trend between the mean scores, from lowest to highest. The fast rate has the lowest mean score, the slow rate the highest mean score, with the medium rate having a mean score in between.

In the examples of one-way ANOVA given in Chapters 14 and 15 the aim was to test the effects of different rates of presentation. The point about ANOVA is that it can only test overall differences between the different presentation rates. The analysis in this chapter makes it possible to investigate the effects of individual experimental conditions on mean scores.

16.3   Comparisons between individual conditions

Let us summarize the argument so far. The first step is to check that there are overall significant differences between the experimental conditions, as revealed by ANOVA tables.

If there are significant overall differences between conditions, a researcher may want to carry out further investigations in order to test comparisons between the individual conditions. The aim is to test whether the scores for individual conditions support the predicted differences in scores.

Because the comparisons between individual conditions are carried out after the main ANOVA analysis, these comparisons are known as *post hoc* comparisons. *Post hoc* is a Latin phrase meaning 'after the event', which tells us that the comparisons are after the original ANOVA.

These comparisons are also called unplanned comparisons. This is because it is only after the means of the individual conditions have been checked that a researcher may decide that it may be worth investigating differences between individual conditions.

16.4   Multiple comparisons between conditions

In order to explore any differences between individual conditions, the researcher needs to test comparisons between pairs of individual conditions. These are often referred to as *multiple comparisons* because several comparisons can be made between pairs of individual conditions. They are sometimes also referred to as *contrasts* because they contrast the effects of pairs of individual conditions.

There are three possible pairs of contrasts between three individual conditions:

Contrast between Condition 1 and Condition 2
Contrast between Condition 2 and Condition 3
Contrast between Condition 1 and Condition 3

One relevant contrast is to test whether the recall scores for Condition 1 (slow rate) are higher than the recall scores for Condition 2 (medium rate). The second relevant contrast is to test whether the recall scores for Condition 2 (medium rate) are higher than the recall scores for Condition 3 (fast rate).

These two contrasts represent the predicted differences in recall scores from highest in Condition 1 (slow) to fewest in Condition 3 (fast). The mean recall scores in the graph in Figure 16.1 reflect the predicted scores, with the highest mean recall scores for C (slow rate).

16.5   Using *t* tests for pairs of conditions

The next question that has to be considered is how to go about testing for contrasts between individual conditions. The basic method is to use *t* tests between each pair of conditions.

You will remember that *t* tests are designed for testing differences between two conditions. This is why *t* tests are ideal for testing comparisons between pairs of individual conditions.

The ANOVA for this experiment was unrelated because groups of different participants were doing each of the three conditions. This means that the appropriate t test for pairs of conditions is the t test (unrelated).

One t test (unrelated) can be used to test the first contrast that scores for slow rates are different from the scores for medium rates. Another t test (unrelated) can be used to test the second contrast that scores for medium rates are different from the scores for fast rates.

16.6   Adjusting significance levels

The need to adjust significance levels arises because several different tests are being carried out on the same data. There is the original ANOVA plus the possibility of three t tests between pairs of scores on individual conditions.

Statistical tests use the conventional level of significance ($p < 0.05$). This represents 1 in 20 probability of random variability. But if a researcher keeps testing the same data, there may be 1 in 20 probability that one of these tests will only appear to be significant. It may be the case that one of the contrasts is accepted as significant even though the scores are random, as stated by the null hypothesis.

To understand what this means we strongly recommend you to look back to Section 4.4, which introduced the notion of one-tailed and two-tailed hypotheses. The point was made that a one-tailed hypothesis predicts differences in scores in conditions in one direction only. A one-tailed hypothesis may have a specific probability of random variance ($p < 0.05$).

A two-tailed hypothesis makes a prediction that the differences in scores in conditions might go in either direction, in favour of either one condition or the other. A two-tailed hypothesis has double the probability of random variance because two hypotheses are being tested, one in one direction and one in the other direction. When a two-tailed hypothesis is being tested, the significance levels have to be adjusted to allow for two hypotheses being tested.

The need for stricter levels of significance for two hypotheses in a two-tailed test applies even more strongly when there are several multiple comparisons between possible pairs of conditions.

It is essential to understand that, if the same significance levels were used for testing all pairs of contrasts between conditions, we would be biasing the analysis in favour of having several goes at obtaining significance based on the same data.

Just as with the two-tailed hypothesis, significance levels have to be stricter, depending on the number of comparisons that are being tested.

The *t* tests for comparisons that we will be describing for testing several contrasts on the same data are based on the general principle that significance levels have to be adjusted for multiple comparisons. The researcher may be interested in testing only one or two of the contrasts between conditions. But from a statistical point of view, other possible contrasts between conditions also have to be taken into account.

16.7 Bonferroni test

The Bonferroni test uses a very direct way of adjusting significance levels in relation to the number of comparisons that could be carried out on three possible contrasts.

The conventional significance level is $p < 0.05$. The Bonferroni approach to obtaining stricter levels of significance is achieved by dividing the 0.05 significance level by the number of possible comparisons. For three contrasts, 0.05 has to be divided by 3, giving 0.017. This represents an adjusted significance level ($p < 0.01$), which applies to all the *t* tests for testing the contrasts between individual conditions. It is necessary to achieve the adjusted significance level of $p < 0.01$ for the *t* tests to be counted as being significant at the conventional $p < 0.05$.

As an example, suppose the calculated *t* test (unrelated) used for testing the contrast between Condition 1 (slow) and Condition 2 (medium) turned out to be $t = 2.65$ ($df = 18$). We need to test this value of *t* at the adjusted significance level ($p < 0.01$). If the adjusted significance level of ($p < 0.01$) is not achieved, the null hypothesis cannot be rejected at the significance level of $p < 0.05$.

In Table C (Statistical Tables at the back of the book) when you look along the row for $df = 18$, the calculated *t* of 2.65 is larger than the adjusted value of 2.552 for one-tail significance ($p < 0.01$). Remember that the researcher can only claim a significant contrast between the recall scores in Condition 1 (slow) and Condition 2 (medium) at the conventional $p < 0.05$.

16.8 Tukey's honestly significant difference

When to use

Tukey's honestly significant difference (HSD) or Q test takes into account all possible contrasts between pairs of conditions. Even if a researcher only wants to test one contrast, the HSD is based on all possible contrasts.

Research hypothesis

The prediction is that there will be differences between individual presentation rates.

Sample data

Table 16.1 gives the overall differences in scores that were analysed in Chapter 14.

These data were tested by a one-way ANOVA (unrelated) because different participants did the three conditions. The overall differences between the three conditions were found to be significant ($p < 0.01$). The only contrast worth investigating in Table 16.1 is the comparison between Condition 2 (medium rate) and Condition 3 (fast rate).

Rationale

The Tukey HSD is used to test differences between pairs of contrasts between individual conditions. The basic method that HSD uses for adjusting for several comparisons on the same data is to take into account the number of conditions that could have been made. The prediction is that there will be relatively large differences between conditions in relation to error variance. If there are random differences between the pairs of individual conditions, as stated by the null hypothesis, the null hypothesis cannot be rejected.

Table 16.1   Number of words recalled for three presentation rates

	Condition 1 (slow rate)	Condition 2 (medium rate)	Condition 3 (fast rate)
	8	7	4
	7	8	5
	9	5	3
	5	4	6
	6	6	2
	8	7	4
Total (T)	43	37	24
Means	7.17	6.17	4

Step-by-step instructions for calculating Tukey's Q

These are given in Box I.

 Box I

Step-by-step instructions for calculating Tukey's Q

1   Note the following symbols   (see Table 16.1)

   M_1 = mean for medium rate $M_1 = 6.17$

   M_2 = mean for fast rate $M_2 = 4$
   (Note that the lower mean has to be
   subtracted from the higher mean)

   n = number of participants in each condition $n = 6$

2   The formula for Q is:

   $$Q = \frac{M_1 - M_2}{\sqrt{\dfrac{MS_{error}}{n}}}$$ $M_1 - M_2 = 6.17 - 4 = 2.17$

   MS_{error} can be found in the original ANOVA $MS_{error} = 2.11$
   (unrelated) in Box G in Chapter 14.

   $$Q = \frac{6.17 - 4}{\sqrt{\dfrac{2.11}{6}}}$$

   $$= \frac{2.17}{\sqrt{0.35}}$$

   $$= \frac{2.17}{0.59}$$

   $$= 3.67$$

Looking up the significance of Q

You can see that the calculation of Q is quite similar to the t test (unrelated) comparing the difference in means against an estimate of total error variance. The difference is in the tables used to test the calculated values of Q. The df are the same as those for the error variance in Box G in Chapter 14 ($df = 15$).

The tables for Q can be found in several textbooks. The Q table is closely based on the t table. The difference is that there is also a column for k, the number of possible contrasts. This means that the number of possible contrasts can be taken into account when calculating significance levels.

In our example $k = 3$ for the three possible contrasts between the three conditions for presentation rates. Because of the stricter requirement for achieving significance, the contrast between Condition 2 (medium rate) and Condition 3 (fast rate) was only just significant ($p < 0.05$).

Conclusions

The contrast between Condition 2 (medium rate) and Condition 3 (fast rate) is significant ($p < 0.05$), taking into account the three possible contrasts that could have been made. The very small difference between the means of Condition 1 and Condition 2 is obviously not significant.

Note about comparisons between conditions in ANOVA (related)

The instructions given in Box I refer to unrelated ANOVA. For ANOVA (related) the principle of taking into account the contrasts that could have been made is the same. Because the ANOVA is related, the comparisons between individual conditions involve carrying out t tests (related), adjusting the significance level depending on the number of contrasts that could have been made.

 Progress box sixteen

- ANOVA tests overall differences.
- Contrasts between individual pairs of conditions can be tested using t tests.
- Because several tests are carried out on the same data, significance levels have to be adjusted.
- Bonferroni and Tukey's HSD are methods for calculating stricter levels of significance.

17 Introduction to two-way ANOVA

17.1 Comparison with one-way ANOVA

In Chapters 14 and 15 you were introduced to one-way ANOVA (unrelated) and one-way ANOVA (related). It was explained that the term 'one-way ANOVA' indicates that there is only one independent variable.

There can be several conditions on one independent variable. An example would be an experiment in which there is one independent variable of three, or even four, different types of word lists.

In this chapter we discuss the possibility of investigating two independent variables. Instead of the experimenter selecting just one independent variable of lists of words, the experimenter will also be able to select a second variable.

Let us take as an example an experiment that tests the effect of a reading scheme on children's reading scores. In one-way ANOVA it would only be possible to investigate one independent variable, either giving the children a reading scheme or not giving them a reading scheme.

In two-way ANOVA two variables can be tested. A second variable could be whether the children are good readers or less good readers.

17.2 Two-way ANOVA

Using two-way ANOVA it is possible to investigate the effects of the reading scheme, the performance of good and less good readers and the crucial question of whether good and less good readers are affected by the reading scheme in different ways.

Two-way ANOVA can test the possibility that there might be a differential effect of one independent variable on another independent variable. This is one of the great advantages of two-way ANOVA. These differential effects are known as *interactions* between the two variables.

Interactions will be fully discussed in the justification for two-way ANOVA experimental designs.

Combining the two variables results in *four* conditions, as shown in Table 17.1. Condition 1 shows the combination of less good readers with no reading scheme; Condition 2, good readers with no reading scheme; Condition 3, less good readers with a reading scheme; and Condition 4, good readers with a reading scheme.

Table 17.1   Four conditions in a two-way ANOVA

Condition 1	*Condition 2*	*Condition 3*	*Condition 4*
Less good readers No reading scheme	Good readers No reading scheme	Less good readers Reading scheme	Good readers Reading scheme

17.3   Two-by-two tables

In order to demonstrate that two-way ANOVA is testing two independent variables, this is usually expressed as a two-by-two table. These are also called 2×2 tables.

In 2×2 tables each of the independent variables is shown separately so that the effects of the two variables can be identified. The 2×2 table in Table 17.2 is another way of displaying the experimental conditions given in Table 17.1.

Table 17.2 shows the effects of two independent variables, each of which has two conditions. The first independent variable is the reading scheme (Variable A: reading scheme or no reading scheme). The second independent variable is reading skills (Variable B: good or less good readers).

The top left-hand box in Table 17.2 represents Condition 1 in Table 17.1: less good readers who are not given a reading scheme. The top right-hand box represents Condition 3: less good readers with a reading scheme.

Boxes in 2×2 tables are usually labelled as *cells* so that there is no need to refer to the 'top left-hand box'. The boxes in Table 17.2 are labelled as cells 1 to 4, as shown in Table 17.3.

Table 17.2 2×2 table for four conditions

Variable B: Reading skills	*Variable A: Reading scheme*	
	No reading scheme	*Reading scheme*
Less good readers	Condition 1	Condition 3
Good readers	Condition 2	Condition 4

Table 17.3 Labelled cells in 2×2 table

	No reading scheme	Reading scheme
Less good readers	Cell 1	Cell 3
Good readers	Cell 2	Cell 4

The next step is to put some numbers into the 2×2 table. Let us suppose that we had carried out an experiment and had recorded scores for each of the four conditions. These scores have been entered into the appropriate cells in Table 17.4.

In Table 17.4 the totals for the Variable A reading scheme conditions and the totals for the Variable B good versus less good readers conditions have also been calculated.

The total for both conditions in which there is no reading scheme adds up the scores for both the less good readers (2) and the good readers (8): $2 + 8 = 10$. The equivalent total for conditions in which there is a reading scheme is the total of less good readers (7) and good readers (8), adding up to 15.

The difference between the totals for no reading scheme (10) and reading scheme (15) shows the overall difference between these two conditions regardless of whether the children were good or less good readers. This overall difference is known as a main effect because it compares the overall scores for Variable A (no reading scheme versus reading scheme).

Table 17.4 2×2 table of score

Variable B   *Variable A*

	No reading scheme	Reading scheme	Totals
Less good readers	2	7	9
Good readers	8	8	16
Totals	10	15	

? **Question 17.1** Which main effect is represented by the totals of 9 and 16 at the right-hand side of Table 17.4?

17.4   Interpreting interactions

It is obviously interesting to look at the main effects in a 2×2 experiment as shown in Table 17.4. These represent the differences between the effects of Variable A, no reading scheme versus reading scheme (total scores of 10 versus 15, showing the main effect of higher scores for the reading scheme). Table 17.4 also shows the differences between Variable B, less good and good readers (9 versus 16, showing the main effect of good readers performing better). However, it could be argued that these main effects could just as well have been demonstrated in two separate experiments. One experiment could have looked at performance with and without the reading scheme. Another experiment could have looked at the performance of less good and good readers.

The whole point of two-way ANOVA is that two independent variables can be investigated simultaneously to see whether the two variables influence each other. What we want to know is whether it is the less good readers or the good readers who benefit most from the reading scheme.

The experimental hypothesis was that less good readers would benefit more from the reading scheme. Good readers are already so good at reading that they would not benefit so much from a reading scheme.

If you look at Table 17.4, it is clear that the overall performance of the good readers is better than the less good readers overall (scores of 16 versus 9). Now look at the individual cells in the table. It is easy to see that the scores for the good readers are no different regardless of whether they had a reading scheme or not (8 versus 8). On the other hand, the less good readers, when given a reading scheme, improved from 2 to 7.

This could be interpreted as showing that good readers are unlikely to show an improvement due to a reading scheme while less good readers are likely to improve their reading performance when they are given a reading scheme. Another way of expressing this is that scores on Variable A (no reading scheme versus reading scheme) are affected by Variable B (good or less good readers).

It is only the less good readers whose performance is affected by the reading scheme. The fact that performance on one variable is affected by performance on the other variable demonstrates that there is an interaction between the two variables.

Interactions are often thought to be a very difficult concept to grasp. But all they mean is that two independent variables interact in the sense that one independent variable is affected by another independent variable. An alternative way of putting this is that participants behave differently on one of the variables as a direct result of the second variable.

17.5 | Using graphs to demonstrate interactions

One good way of indicating whether there is an interaction between variables is to draw a graph of the data. In Figure 17.1 the vertical axis is labelled Reading scores. The horizontal axis is labelled No reading scheme and Reading scheme.

The aim is to plot the reading scores of the less good and good readers against the no reading scheme and reading scheme conditions. We use the total scores in Table 17.4. For good readers the reading scores were 8 for both the no reading scheme and reading scheme conditions. Scores for good readers are both plotted against the score of 8 on the reading scores vertical axis.

For less good readers the reading scores were 2 for no reading scheme and 7 for the reading scheme, so for less good readers their reading scores are plotted at 2 and 7 on the vertical axis.

In order to demonstrate whether there is an interaction the normal practice is to draw lines connecting the reading scores for good and less good readers. The line connecting the reading scores for the good readers is flat because good readers got exactly the same score whether they were given a reading scheme or not.

In contrast, the line connecting the scores for less good readers shows a definite slope, rising from 2 for the no reading scheme condition to 7 for

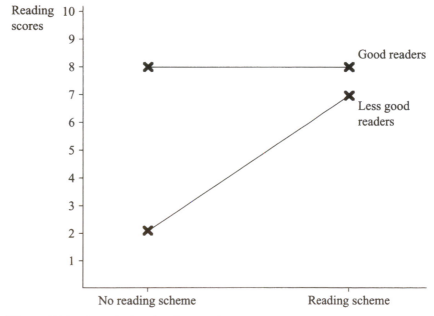

Figure 17.1   Graph showing interaction

the reading scheme condition. The rising line demonstrates an improvement in reading scores for the less good readers. These lines indicate that there is quite likely to be an interaction between the amount of improvement of good readers and less good readers.

We will now give another example where there is no interaction. Different scores for the four conditions are shown in Table 17.5. The scores in Table 17.5 are plotted on the graph in Figure 17.2.

In the graph in Figure 17.2 good readers have higher reading scores than less good readers (13 versus 9). But in this case both good readers and less good readers benefit from the reading scheme.

The less good readers improve from 2 to 7 and the good readers improve from 4 to 9. These equal rates of improvements are shown in Figure 17.2 as the same slopes for both good and less good readers.

Table 17.5 2×2 table of scores

	No reading scheme	*Reading scheme*	Totals
Less good readers	2	7	9
Good readers	4	9	13
Totals	6	16	

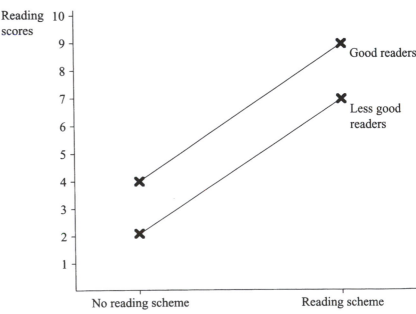

Figure 17.2   Graph showing no interaction

These equal slopes indicate that there is no hint of any interaction between the two variables. Both groups of readers have shown the same amount of improvement from the reading scheme.

You will probably have realized by now that a graph is simply another way of representing a 2 × 2 table. The graph in Figure 17.1 is equivalent to the 2 × 2 table of scores in Table 17.4. The graph in Figure 17.2 is equivalent to the 2 × 2 table of scores in Table 17.5.

 Progress box seventeen

- In one-way ANOVA only one independent variable (IV) can be tested.
- In two-way ANOVA two IVs can be tested simultaneously.
- Main effects can be identified for each IV separately.
- Interactions occur when different values of one IV affect performance on a second IV.
- Graphs are a good method for demonstrating interactions.

Two-way ANOVA (unrelated)

18.1 Scores from different participants

In two-way ANOVA (unrelated) different participants do each condition. Because different participants do only one of the experimental conditions, it is not possible to calculate variance by comparing related scores for each participant.

In two-way ANOVA two independent variables (IVs) are tested. In two-way ANOVA (unrelated) two groups of different participants do the two conditions on one independent variable, while two groups of different participants do the two conditions on the other independent variable. Thus there are four groups in all.

An example would be an experiment in which the first IV is a comparison between learning lists of long or short words. The second IV is a comparison between fast and slow rates of presenting the lists of words, as shown below.

Variable A (length of words)
Condition A_1 (short words)
Condition A_2 (long words)

Variable B (presentation rates)
Condition B_1 (fast rate)
Condition B_2 (slow rate)

Two groups of different participants will be doing the two Variable A conditions (length of words). Two other groups of different participants will be doing the two Variable B conditions (presentation rates).

This means that there will be four groups of different participants each doing one of the four combinations listed in Table 18.1. We have indicated this by showing the four different groups each doing one of the four conditions.

Table 18.1 Four groups of different participants doing four conditions

Group 1 Short words (A_1) presented at a fast rate (B_1)
Group 2 Short words (A_1) presented at a slow rate (B_2)
Group 3 Long words (A_2) presented at a fast rate B_1)
Group 4 Long words (A_2) presented at a slow rate (B_2)

? Question 18.1 Suppose Variable A is a comparison between illustrated texts (A_1) and non-illustrated texts (A_2). Variable B is a comparison between texts with a title (B_1) and texts with no title (B_2).

Following the example in Table 18.1, fill in the combinations of the two variables for four groups of different participants.

Group 1
Group 2
Group 3
Group 4

18.2 Definitions of variances

For two-way ANOVA (unrelated), when there are two independent variables, there are five sources of variance that can be calculated:

Between conditions on Variable A (predicted)
Between conditions on Variable B (predicted)
Interaction between A and B (predicted), which are denoted by A × B
Error variance (due to irrelevant variables, including individual differences between participants)
Total variance (including all the above sources of variance)

18.3 Selecting a statistical test in the Decision Chart

Differences between conditions?
The answer to this question is 'Yes' because the aim of the experiment is to test predicted differences between experimental conditions.

One or two variables?
The answer for two-way ANOVA is two variables.

Related or unrelated design?

The answer is unrelated design because different participants are doing each condition.

You will find that if you answered the above three questions in the Decision Chart as suggested, you will arrive at two-way ANOVA (unrelated). This is the appropriate parametric test for a two-way unrelated design testing two independent variables.

18.4   Using two-way ANOVA (unrelated)

When to use

Two-way ANOVA (unrelated) should be used for an unrelated design when different participants are doing two conditions on two independent variables and the data are interval.

Research hypothesis

It was predicted that there would be an interaction between Variable A and Variable B. More short words would be recalled at a fast rate of presentation and more long words at a slow rate of presentation.

Sample data

Four groups of four different participants are allocated to the four combinations of Variable A conditions and Variable B conditions. The scores and means are shown in Table 18.2.

Table 18.2   Recall score for four participants on each condition

	A_1 (short words)		A_2 (long words)	
	B_1 (fast rate)	B_2 (slow rate)	B_1 (fast rate)	B_2 (slow rate)
	9	4	5	7
	8	3	3	5
	6	3	3	6
	7	5	4	7
Means	7.5	3.75	3.75	6.25

The scores in Table 18.2 are entered into four cells as shown in Table 18.3.

Table 18.3 Recall scores for two variables (unrelated)

Variable B (rate of presentation)	Variable A (word length)		Totals B
	A_1 (short words)	A_2 (long words)	
B_1 (fast rate)	9 8 6 7	5 3 3 4	
	30	15	45
B_2 (slow rate)	4 3 3 5	7 5 6 7	
	15	25	40
			Grand total
Totals A	45	40	85

Notes on Table 18.3

1 Four scores are shown for the four participants in each cell of the table. There are four participants in cell A_1B_1; four different participants in cell A_1B_2; four different participants in cell A_2B_1; four different participants in cell A_2B_2.

2 The totals have been added for the four scores in each cell.

3 The total scores for the two Variable A conditions have been added (along the bottom line) and the total scores for the two Variable B conditions (at the right-hand side).

4 These totals have been added to produce a grand total of 85.

Rationale

The aim of ANOVA is to compare ratios of variance. The between-conditions variance for Variable A, Variable B and the interaction $A \times B$ represent predicted variances between conditions. Differences in scores due to irrelevant variables represent error variance. The prediction is that there will be relatively large differences between conditions compared with error variance. If there are random differences between conditions, as stated by the null hypothesis, the predicted differences between conditions will be small in relation to error variance. In this case, the null hypothesis cannot be rejected.

Step-by-step instructions for calculating two-way ANOVA (unrelated)

These are given in Box J.

 Box J

Step-by-step instructions for calculating 2×2 *F* ratios (unrelated)

1   Note the following symbols (see Table 18.3):

$\sum T_a^2$ = sum of A squared totals $\sum T_a^2 = 45^2 + 40^2$

$\sum T_b^2$ = sum of B squared totals $\sum T_b^2 = 45^2 + 40^2$

$\sum T_{ab}^2$ = the sum of AB squared totals $\sum T_{ab}^2 = 30^2 + 15^2 + 15^2 + 25^2$

$\quad n$ = number of subjects in each condition $n = 4$

$\quad a$ = number of conditions for variable A $a = 2$

$\quad b$ = number of conditions for variable B $b = 2$

$\quad N$ = total number of scores $N = 16$

$(\sum x)^2$ = grand total squared $(\sum x)^2 = 85^2$

$\dfrac{(\sum x)^2}{N}$ = constant to be subtracted from all SS $\dfrac{85^2}{16} = 451.5625$

$\quad \sum x^2$ = sum of each individual score squared

2   Calculate SS_A

$$\frac{\sum T_a^2}{nb} - \frac{(\sum x)^2}{N}$$

$$= \frac{45^2 + 40^2}{4 \times 2} - 451.5625$$

$$= 453.125 - 451.5625$$

$$= 1.5625$$

3   Calculate SS_B

$$\frac{\sum T_b^2}{na} - \frac{(\sum x)^2}{N}$$

$$= \frac{45^2 + 40^2}{4 \times 2} - 451.5625$$

$$= 453.125 - 451.5625$$

$$= 1.5625$$

4   Calculate SS_{AB}

$$\frac{\sum T_{ab}^2}{n} - \frac{(\sum x)^2}{N} - SS_A - SS_B$$

$$= \frac{30^2 + 15^2 + 15^2 + 25^2}{4}$$

$$- 451.5625 - 1.5625$$

$$- 1.5625$$

Note that you have already calculated SS_A and SS_B and the constant.

$= 493.75 - 451.5625$
$- 1.5625 - 1.5625$
$= 39.0625$

5　Calculate SS_{tot}

$$\sum x^2 - \frac{(\sum x)^2}{N}$$

$= 9^2 + 8^2 + 6^2 + 7^2$ plus all other individual scores squared $- 451.5625$
$= 507 - 451.5625$
$= 55.4375$

6　Calculate SS_{error}
$SS_{tot} - SS_A - SS_B - SS_{AB}$

$= 55.4375 - 1.5625$
$- 1.5625 - 39.0625$
$= 13.25$

7　Calculate the degrees of freedom

df_A = number of A conditions minus 1　　$df_A = 2 - 1 = 1$
df_B = number of B conditions minus 1　　$df_B = 2 - 1 = 1$
$df_{AB} = df_A \times df_B$　　$df_{AB} = 1 \times 1 = 1$
$df_{tot} = N - 1$　　$df_{tot} = 16 - 1 = 15$
$df_{error} = df_{tot} - df_A - df_B - df_{AB}$　　$df_{error} = 15 - 1 - 1 - 1 = 12$

8　Divide each SS by df to obtain MS

$$MS_A = \frac{SS_A}{df_A}$$　　$MS_A = 1.5625$

$$MS_B = \frac{SS_B}{df_B}$$　　$MS_B = 1.5625$

$$MS_{AB} = \frac{SS_{AB}}{df_{AB}}$$　　$MS_{AB} = 39.0625$

$$MS_{error} = \frac{SS_{error}}{df_{error}}$$　　$MS_{error} = 1.104$

9　Calculate F ratios for MS_A, MS_B and MS_{AB} allocating the correct df to the F ratios

$$F \text{ ratio for } MS_A = \frac{MS_A}{MS_{error}}$$　　$F_{1,12} = 1.415$

$$F \text{ ratio for } MS_B = \frac{MS_B}{MS_{error}}$$　　$F_{1,12} = 1.415$

$$F \text{ ratio for } MS_{AB} = \frac{MS_{AB}}{MS_{error}}$$　　$F_{1,12} = 35.38$

10　The completed ANOVA table is shown in Table 18.4

Notes on calculations in Box J

1 Note the definitions of the symbols and the calculation of the constant, which is to be subtracted from all sums of squares.
2 SS_A is based on the two Variable A totals shown in Table 18.3.
3 SS_B is based on the two Variable B totals shown in Table 18.3.
4 SS_{AB} is based on the totals of the four scores in each cell in Table 18.3 minus SS_A and SS_B and, of course, the constant.
5 Total variance (SS_{tot}) is calculated from all the individual scores.
6 SS_{error} is calculated by subtracting all the other variances from SS_{tot}.
7 Calculate the *df* as instructed. The only point to notice is that df_{AB} is the result of multiplying df_A by df_B.
8 *MS* values are calculated by dividing *SS* by the relevant *df*.
9 *F* ratios are calculated by dividing the three predicted *MS* variances of A, B and A × B by MS error.

Table 18.4   Two-way ANOVA table (unrelated)

Sources of variance	Sums of squares	Degrees of freedom	Mean squares	F ratios
Variable A (word length)	1.5625	1	1.5625	$F_{1,12} = 1.415$
Variable B (presentation rate)	1.5625	1	1.5625	$F_{1,12} = 1.415$
$A \times B$ (interaction)	39.0625	1	39.0625	$F_{1,12} = 35.38$
Error	13.25	12	1.104	
Total	55.4375	15		

Looking up the significance of *F* in Table G

Tables G(1) and G(2) are the appropriate tables for all ANOVA tests. Table G(1) gives the critical vales for $p < 0.05$. Table G(2) gives the critical values for $p < 0.01$. The calculated *F* has to be equal to or larger than the critical values. You need to use the degrees of freedom for all three between-conditions variances A, B, AB, and the error variance. You can use the *df* from step 7 in Box J (in our example $df_A = 1$, $df_B = 1$, df_{AB} 1, $df_{error} = 12$). What makes this easier is that all the variances have the same *df*. So we only have to look up the values for $df = 1,12$.

   In Table G(1) *df* for variables A,B,AB, is shown along the v_1 row and *df* error is shown down the v_2 column. Locate 1 on v_1 along the top line and follow the v_2 column down until you find 12. Where they intersect is the critical value for $F_{1,12}$ of 4.75 ($p < 0.05$). The calculated *F* for *A* and *B* of 1.415 is obviously much smaller than 4.75. But the calculated *F* for the $A \times B$ interaction of 35.38 is larger than the critical value of 4.75. The

F of 35.38 is also larger than the critical value in Table G(2) for $df = 1,12$ of 9.33. So the null hypothesis for the $A \times B$ interaction can be rejected ($p < 0.01$).

Conclusions

The $A \times B$ interaction between Variable A and Variable B is significant ($p < 0.01$). If we look at the means in Table 18.2, it is clear that there are higher means for short words at a fast rate (7.5) and for long words at a slow rate (6.25). One possible reason for this significant $A \times B$ interaction is that long words take longer to memorize and so benefit from a slow rate of presentation. Short words take less time and so with a slow rate they may be forgotten. Short words are likely to benefit from a faster rate of presentation.

18.5 Using graphs

Interactions are often demonstrated by graphs. The output of an SPSS computer program is an ANOVA table (see Table 18.4) and usually a graph as well. But it is useful to plot a graph for yourself in order to understand the significance of an interaction.

In the graph in Figure 18.1 the fast rate and slow rate are shown along the bottom line. Lines are drawn to plot long words and short words against the mean recall scores, which are repeated below.

Mean for short words at fast rate   7.5
Mean for short words at slow rate   3.75
Mean for long words at fast rate   3.75
Mean for long words at slow rate   6.25

The fact that the lines in Figure 18.1 cross over is an indication of the interaction between the two IVs of short/long words and fast/slow presentation rates. The variable of rate presentation affects the recall scores on short and long words in opposite directions. More short words are recalled with a fast rate and more long words at a slow rate.

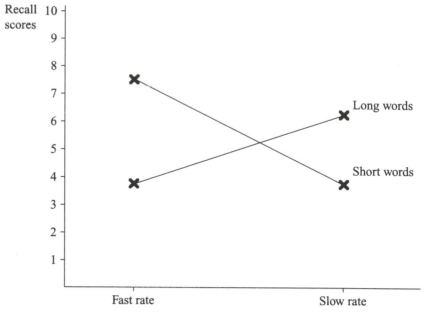

Figure 18.1   Graph for 2×2 ANOVA (unrelated)

▶ **Progress box eighteen**

- In two-way ANOVA (unrelated) there are two independent variables.
- In two-way ANOVA (unrelated) the scores on four conditions for the two IVs are produced by different participants.
- Five sources of variance are tested by two-way ANOVA (unrelated): between conditions on Variable *A*; between conditions on Variable *B*; interaction between *A* and *B* ($A \times B$); error variance; and total variance.
- The appropriate parametric statistical test for analysing the five sources of variance is two-way ANOVA (unrelated).

Two-way ANOVA (related)

Scores from same participants

In two-way ANOVA (related) the same participants do all the conditions. Because each participant produces scores on all the conditions, the scores for each participant are related. By calculating the differences between participants' related scores, it is possible to calculate individual variance for participants.

In two-way ANOVA two independent variables (IVs) are tested. In two-way ANOVA (related) the same participants do the two conditions on one variable and also do the two conditions on the other variable.

An example would be an experiment in which the first IV is a comparison between learning lists of long or short words. The second IV is a comparison between fast and slow rates of presenting the lists of words, as shown below.

Variable A (length of words)
Condition A_1 (short words)
Condition A_2 (long words)

Variable B (presentation rates)
Condition B_1 (fast rate)
Condition B_2 (slow rate)

In two-way ANOVA (related) the same participants will be doing the two conditions on Variable A and also the two conditions on Variable B. The same participants will be doing all four conditions listed in Table 19.1.

Table 19.1   Same participants doing all four conditions

Condition 1   Short words (A_1) presented at a fast rate (B_1)
Condition 2   Short words (A_1) presented at a slow rate (B_2)
Condition 3   Long words (A_2) presented at a fast rate B_1)
Condition 4   Long words (A_2) presented at a slow rate (B_2)

? Question 19.1   Suppose Variable A is a comparison between illustrated texts (A_1) and non-illustrated texts (A_2). Variable B is a comparison between texts with a title (B_1) and texts with no title (B_2).

Following the example in Table 19.1, fill in the four conditions on the two variables, which are all done by the same participants.

Condition 1
Condition 2
Condition 3
Condition 4

19.2   Definitions of variances

Two-way ANOVA (related) indicates that there are two independent variables.

For two-way ANOVA (related) there are several extra sources of variance. The reason for this is that for a related design it is possible to calculate individual variance between participants. This is based on the differences between each participant's related scores. Thus as many as eight sources of variance can be calculated. These include:

Between conditions on Variable A (predicted)
Between conditions on Variable B (predicted)
Interaction between A and B (predicted)
Variance S (based on differences between participants' related scores)
Error $A \times S$ (interaction between Variable A and S variance)
Error $B \times S$ (interaction between Variable B and S variance)
Error $A \times B \times S$ (three-way interaction between Variable A, Variable B and S variance)
Total variance (including all the above sources of variance)

Note that it is universal in all statistical textbooks to use the term S (for subjects) and not P for participants.

19.3 Selecting a statistical test in the Decision Chart

Differences between conditions?
The answer to this question is 'Yes' because the aim of the experiment is to test predicted differences between experimental conditions.

One or two variables?
The answer for two-way ANOVA is two variables.

Related or unrelated design?
The answer is related design because the same participants are doing all four conditionis on two variables.

You will find that if you answered the above three questions in the Decision Chart as suggested, you will arrive at two-way ANOVA (related). This is the appropriate parametric test for a two-way related design testing two independent variables.

19.4 Using two-way ANOVA (related)

When to use

Two-way ANOVA (related) should be used for a related design when the same participants are doing all conditions on two independent variables and the data are interval.

Research hypothesis

It was predicted that there would be significant effects of Variable A between long and short words and Variable B between fast and slow rates of presenting the word lists. No interaction was predicted between the two variables.

Sample data

The same four participants are allocated to the four combinations of Variable A conditions and Variable B conditions. This means that each participant will have four scores in the four conditions, amounting to 16 scores in all. These scores and means are shown in Table 19.2.

Table 19.2   Recall scores for two variables (related)

	A_1 (short words)		A_2 (long words)	
Participants	B_1 (fast rate)	B_2 (slow rate)	B_1 (fast rate)	B_2 (slow rate)
1	7	7	3	5
2	5	6	1	3
3	6	8	2	5
4	4	9	2	4
Means	5.5	7.5	2	4.25

Because there are so many sources of variances and interactions for ANOVA (related) the data in Table 19.2 have to be shown in three separate tables of cells. These tables represent summaries of the same data in different combinations: A, B and $A \times B$ interaction (Table 19.3); A, S and $A \times S$ interaction (Table 19.4); and B, S and $B \times S$ interaction (Table 19.5).

Table 19.3   *AB* summary table

	A_1		A_2		Totals B (T_b)
B_1	7 5		3 1		
	6 4		2 2		
		22		8	30
B_2	7 6		5 3		
	8 9		5 4		
		30		17	47
Totals A (T_a)		52		25	77 Grand total

Notes on Table 19.3

1 This table has the same structure of Variable A and Variable B cells as Table 18.3 in Chapter 18.

2 The totals are added for the scores in the four cells and the totals of A and B, adding up to the grand total of 77.

Table 19.4 *AS* summary table

	A_1		A_2		*Totals S* (T_s)
S_1	7	7	3	5	
		14		8	22
S_2	5	6	1	3	
		11		4	15
S_3	6	8	2	5	
		14		7	21
S_4	4	9	2	4	
		13		6	19
Totals A (T_a)	52		25		77 Grand total

Notes on Table 19.4
1 This table shows the related scores for each participant (S) on the two Variable A conditions.
2 The related scores for each participant are added as Totals S on the right-hand side of the table.
3 The totals for A are the same as in Table 19.3.
4 All the scores in each summary table add up to the grand total of 77.

Table 19.5   *BS* summary table

	B_1		B_2		*Totals S (T_s)*
S_1	7	3	7	5	
		10		12	22
S_2	5	1	6	3	
		6		9	15
S_3	6	2	8	5	
		8		13	21
S_4	4	2	9	4	
		6		13	19
Totals *B* (T_b)		30		47	77 Grand total

Notes on Table 19.5

1 This table shows the related scores for each participant (S) on the two Variable B conditions.
2 The related scores for each participant for Totals S are the same as in Table 19.4.
3 The totals for B are the same as in Table 19.3.
4 All the scores in each summary table add up to the grand total of 77.

Rationale

The aim of ANOVA is to compare ratios of variance. The between-conditions variance for Variable A, Variable B and the interaction $A \times B$ represent predicted variances between conditions. Differences in scores due to irrelevant variables represent error variance. The prediction is that there will be relatively large differences between conditions compared with error variance. If there are random differences between conditions, as stated by the null hypothesis, the predicted differences between conditions will be small in relation to error variance. In this case, the null hypothesis cannot be rejected.

Step-by-step instructions for calculating two-way ANOVA (related).

These are given in Box K.

 Box K

Step-by-step instructions for calculating 2×2 *F* ratios (related)

1 Note the following symbols
(see Tables 19.3–19.5):

$\sum T_a^2$ = sum of *A* squared totals Table 19.3 $\sum T_a^2 = 52^2 + 25^2$

$\sum T_b^2$ = sum of *B* squared totals Table 19.3 $\sum T_b^2 = 30^2 + 47^2$

$\sum T_{ab}^2$ = sum of *AB* squared totals for individual cells in Table 19.3 $\sum T_{ab}^2 = 22^2 + 30^2 + 8^2 + 17^2$

$\sum T_s^2$ = sum of squared totals for each participant Table 19.4 $\sum T_s^2 = 22^2 + 15^2 + 21^2 + 19^2$

$\sum T_{as}^2$ = sum of *AS* squared totals for individual cells in Table 19.4 $\sum T_{as}^2 = 14^2 + 11^2 + 14^2 + 13^2 + 8^2 + 4^2 + 7^2 + 6^2$

$\sum T_{bs}^2$ = sum of *BS* squared totals for the individual cells in Table 19.5 $\sum T_{bs}^2 = 10^2 + 6^2 + 8^2 + 6^2 + 12^2 + 9^2 + 13^2 + 13^2$

n = numbers of participants $n = 4$

a = number of conditions for variable *A* $a = 2$

b = number of conditions for variable *B* $b = 2$

N = total number of scores $N = 16$

$(\sum x)^2$ = grand total squared $(\sum x)^2 = 77^2$

$\dfrac{(\sum x)^2}{N}$ = constant to be subtracted from all SS $= \dfrac{77^2}{16} = 370.5625$

$\sum x^2$ = sum of each individual score squared $\sum x^2 = 449$

2   Calculate SS_A

$$\frac{\sum T_a^2}{nb} - \frac{(\sum x)^2}{N}$$ $= 45.5625$

3   Calculate SS_B

$$\frac{\sum T_b^2}{na} - \frac{(\sum x)^2}{N}$$ $= 18.0625$

4   Calculate SS_S

$$\frac{\sum T_s^2}{ab} - \frac{(\sum x)^2}{N}$$ $$= \frac{22^2 + 15^2 + 21^2 + 19^2}{4} - 370.5625$$
$$= 377.75 - 370.5625$$
$$= 7.1875$$

5   Calculate SS_{AB}

$$\frac{\sum T_{ab}^2}{n} - \frac{(\sum x)^2}{N} - SS_A - SS_B$$ $$= \frac{22^2 + 30^2 + 8^2 + 17^2}{4}$$
$$= 0.0625$$

6   Calculate SS_{AS}

$$\frac{\sum T_{as}^2}{b} - \frac{(\sum x)^2}{N} - SS_A - SS_S$$ $$= \frac{14^2 + 11^2 + 14^2 + 13^2 + 8^2 + 4^2 + 7^2 + 6^2}{2}$$
$$- 370.5625 - 45.5625 - 7.1875$$
$$= 423.5 - 370.5625 - 45.5625 - 7.1875$$
$$= 0.1875$$

7   Calculate SS_{BS}

$$\frac{\sum T_{bs}^2}{a} - \frac{(\sum x)^2}{N} - SS_B - SS_S$$ $$= \frac{10^2 + 6^2 + 8^2 + 6^2 + 12^2 + 9^2 + 13^2 + 13^2}{2}$$
$$- 370.5625 - 18.0625 - 7.1875$$
$$= 399.5 - 370.5625 - 18.0625 - 7.1875$$
$$= 3.6875$$

8   Calculate SS_{tot}

$$\sum x^2 - \frac{(\sum x)^2}{N}$$ $= 78.4375$

9   Calculate SS_{ABS}

$$SS_{tot} - SS_A - SS_B - SS_S$$
$$- SS_{AB} - SS_{AS} - SS_{BS}$$ $$= 78.4375 - 45.5625 - 18.0625 - 7.1875$$
$$- 0.0625 - 0.1875 - 3.6875$$
$$= 3.6875$$

10   Calculate the degrees of freedom

$$df_A = 2 - 1 = 1$$
$$df_B = 2 - 1 = 1$$
$$df_S = 4 - 1 = 3$$
$$df_{AB} = 1 \times 1 = 1$$
$$df_{AS} = 1 \times 3 = 3$$
$$df_{BS} = 1 \times 3 = 3$$
$$df_{ABS} = 1 \times 1 \times 3 = 3$$
$$df_{tot} = 16 - 1 = 15$$

11   Divide each *SS* by *df* to obtain *MS*

12   Calculate *F* ratios allocating correct *df* to each *F* ratio

$$F \text{ ratio for } MS_A = \frac{MS_A}{MS_{AS}} \qquad F_{1,3} = 729$$

$$F \text{ ratio for } MS_B = \frac{MS_B}{MS_{BS}} \qquad F_{1,3} = 14.7$$

$$F \text{ ratio for } MS_{AB} = \frac{MS_{AB}}{MS_{ABS}} \qquad F_{1,3} = 0.051$$

$$F \text{ ratio for } MS_S = \frac{MS_S}{MS_{ABS}} \qquad F_{3,3} = 1.95$$

13   The completed ANOVA table is shown in Table 19.6

Notes on calculations in Box K

1 Note the definitions and numerical examples of the symbols and the calculation of the constant, which will be subtracted from each *SS*.

2 The formulae for SS_A, SS_B and SS_{AB} are familiar from Box J in Chapter 18. SS_A is based on the two squared totals for A in Table 19.3. SS_B is based on the two squared totals for B in Table 19.3. SS_{AB} is based on the totals of the squared scores in the cells in Table 19.3.

3 SS_S is a new source of variance based on the squared totals for T_s in Table 19.4.

4 SS_{AS} is a new equation for error based on the squared totals of the cells in Table 19.4.

5 SS_{BS} is a new equation for error based on the squared totals of the cells in Table 19.5.

6 SS_{tot} is based on the squares of all the individual scores in Table 19.3 minus the constant

7 SS_{ABS} is error calculated by subtracting all the other calculated sums of squares from SS_{tot}.

8 Follow the instructions for calculating the rather complicated *df* for each source of variance.

9 The *F* ratios are calculated by using the calculated error which is appropriate for each source of variance. MS_A is compared with *AS* error, MS_B with *BS* error, and MS_{AB} with *ABS* error. MS_S is also compared with *ABS* error.

Table 19.6   Two-way ANOVA table (related)

Sources of variance	Sums of squares	Degrees of freedom	Mean squares	F ratios
Variable *A* (word length)	45.5625	1	45.5625	$F_{1,3} = 729$
Variable *B* (presentation rate)	18.0625	1	18.0625	$F_{1,3} = 14.7$
S (subjects)	7.1875	3	2.3958	$F_{3,3} = 1.95$
A × *B* (interaction)	0.0625	1	0.0625	$F_{1,3} = 0.051$
Error *AS*	0.1875	3	0.0625	
Error *BS*	3.6875	3	1.229	
Error *ABS*	3.6875	3	1.229	
Total	78.4375	15		

Looking up the significance of *F* in Table G

Tables G(1) and G(2) are the appropriate tables for all ANOVA tests. Table G(1) gives the critical values for $p < 0.05$. Table G(2) gives the critical values for $p < 0.01$. The calculated *F* has to be equal to or larger than the critical values. You need to use the degrees of freedom for all three between-conditions variances for *A*, *B*, *AB*, and the error variances. You can use the *df* from step 10 in Box K (in our example $df_A = 1$ and $df_{AS} = 3$; $df_B = 1$ and $df_{BS} = 3$; $df_{AB} = 1$ and $df_{ABS} = 3$. What makes this easier is that all the variances have the same *df* 1,3. So we only have to look up the critical values for *df* = 1,3. You will note that there is no row in. Table G for *df* as low as 3. In this case, it is usual to use the *df* = 5 row.

In Table G(1) *df* for A, B, AB, is shown along the v_1 row and *df* error is shown down the v_2 column. Locate 1 on v_1 along the top line and follow the v_2 column down until you find 5. Where they intersect is the critical value of 6.61. The calculated F for A of 729 in Box K is much larger than this critical value and it is also larger than the critical value in Table G(2) for $df = 1,5$ of 16.26. So the null hypothesis for Variable A can be rejected ($p < 0.01$). The calculated F for B of 14.7 is larger than the critical value of 6.61 in Table G(1) but smaller than the critical value of 16.26 in Table G(2). So the null hypothesis for Variable B can be rejected ($p < 0.05$).

The calculated F for $A \times B$ of 0.051 is obviously too small so the null hypothesis for the $A \times B$ interaction cannot be rejected. It is common practice to test the significance of the F for S variance, hoping that individual differences between participants will not be a significant source of variance. In our example, the calculated F of 1.95 ($df = 3,3$) is smaller than the critical value in Table G(1). So the differences between participants (S) are not significant.

Conclusions

If you look at the means in Table 19.2, you will find that, as predicted, significantly more short words were recalled than long words and more words recalled at a slow rate than a fast rate. These are main effects of the two variables separately (see discussion of main effects in Chapter 17, Section 17.3). There was no significant interaction between the two variables and the differences between participants were not significant.

19.5 Using the SPSS computer program

The calculation of so many different sources of error variance is much more complicated for ANOVA (related). It is likely that that you may have access to a computer program like SPSS to help you with the actual calculations.

Inputs to SPSS computer statistical packages for ANOVA (related)

The scores for the four conditions will have to be input to SPSS, indicating that the scores come from the same participants. This will help you to understand which scores from Tables 19.3, 19.4 and 19.5 you should be inputting to the computer.

Outputs of SPSS computer packages for ANOVA (related)

The main output will be in the form of an ANOVA (related) table as in Table 19.6.

The other output will be a graph showing the relationships between the variables, as in Figure 19.1.

In Figure 19.1 fast rate and slow rate are printed at the bottom of the graph and the short words and long words are plotted against the mean recall scores.

The two parallel lines in Figure 19.1 show that short words had bigger mean recall scores than long words. However, there is no interaction between the two variables of short and long words and fast and slow presentation rates because neither variable has any effect on the other variable.

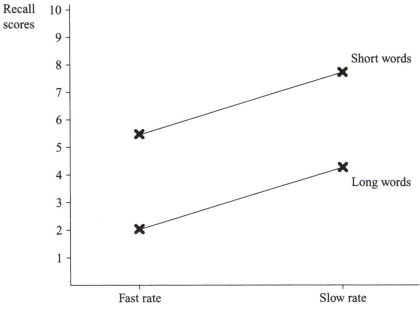

Figure 19.1　Graph for 2 × 2 ANOVA (related)

19.6　Note about mixed designs

It is possible to use a mixed ANOVA design. What is meant by a mixed ANOVA design is that it is a mixture between same participants and different participants.

There are still two variables in the experiment, Variable A and Variable B. The difference is that the same participants do both conditions on Variable A, while different participants do each condition on Variable B.

An example would be that the same four participants learn both short words and long words (Variable A). This would control for possible individual differences between participants' learning ability.

Different groups of participants would be presented with the lists of words at a slow rate or a fast rate (Variable B). Different participants might be selected because participants might be affected by being exposed to two different rates of presentation.

A mixed design is shown in Table 19.7.

Table 19.7   Example of a mixed design

		A_1 (short words)	A_2 (long words)	Totals S (T_s)	Totals A (T_a)
B_1 (fast rate)	P_1	8	4	12	
	P_2	7	4	11	
	P_3	7	5	12	
		22	13		35
B_2 (slow rate)	P_4	4	4	8	
	P_5	6	7	13	
	P_6	7	5	12	
		17	16		33
Totals B (T_b)		39	29		68 Grand total

Notes on Table 19.7
1 Six participants took part in this mixed design.
2 All of the six participants did both the A_1 and the A_2 conditions. They produced a pair of related scores for short words and for long words.
3 Two different groups of three participants did the B_1 and B_2 conditions. The scores for fast and slow rates were unrelated.

We have given you only a very brief introduction to mixed ANOVA with a mixture of same participants and different participants on the two independent variables. If you want to select a mixed ANOVA you will have to ask advice. Alternatively, you can use the appropriate SPSS computer program.

Progress box nineteen

- In two-way ANOVA (related) there are two independent variables. The scores in four conditions on the two variables are produced by the same participants.
- Eight sources of variance are tested by two-way ANOVA (related). The five main sources include:

  Between conditions on Variable A
  Between conditions on Variable B
  Interaction $A \times B$ (AB)
  Individual variance (S)
  Total variance

- The other three variances are accounted for by these variances in interaction with S variance, some of which constitute different types of error.

  Interaction $A \times S$ (error AS)
  Interaction $B \times S$ (error BS)
  Interaction $A \times B \times S$ (error ABS)

- The appropriate parametric statistical test for analysing these eight sources of variance is two-way ANOVA (related).

- It is possible to use a mixed design in which one variable is related and the other variable is unrelated.

Part IV   Relationships between variables

20 Chi-square

20.1 Comparison with experiments

In Chapter 1 we introduced the idea that all psychological research is concerned with testing relationships between variables. In Chapter 2 experiments were introduced as a special case of relationships between variables. Experimenters manipulate independent variables and predict the outcome in terms of effects on measured dependent variables. This makes it possible to predict differences between experimental conditions.

All the statistical tests that were introduced in Parts II and III were designed to test data from experiments. The non-parametric tests and the parametric tests, including ANOVA, are all designed to test differences between conditions.

In psychological research a researcher tests a hypothesis about relationships between variables. The only issue is how much control the researcher has over the variables in the design.

20.2 Measuring categories

The essential characteristic of chi-square is that it does not deal at all with scores. Both variables are represented as categories. This means that for chi-square the only measure of participants' behaviour on both variables is what categories participants are allocated to.

An example might be to observe whether participants are more likely to be able to solve a problem if they are given a hint. The measure is how many people can solve the problem with and without a hint.

For the chi-square test it is only appropriate to count the number of participants who solve the problem and the number of participants who do not solve the problem. It is absolutely crucial to understand that the times taken to solve the problem are not relevant. The only relevant measure is whether participants fall into the category of solving the problem or into the category of not solving the problem.

20.3 Nominal data

Because the number of participants in each *category* is the relevant measure, this kind of measure is known as *nominal* data. The use of the term 'nominal' emphasizes that that this type of measurement can only give a label, or *name*, to the categories. This is completely distinct from the *scores* used in other kinds of research.

In our experiment the names (labels) given to categories are as follows:

Variable *A* Giving hints
Category 1 Giving a hint
Category 2 No hint

Variable *B* Solving problems
Category 1 Solving a problem
Category 2 Not solving a problem.

Another term that is sometimes used for nominal data is *categorical* data. This term is used because data are measured as the number of participants in each category.

? Question 20.1 A researcher gave one group of participants instructions about the advantages of helping strangers and another group of participants warnings about the possible dangers of helping strangers (Variable *A*). The measure was counting the numbers of participants who were observed helping a stranger or not helping a stranger (Variable *B*).

(a) What were the two categories for Variable *A*?

(b) What were the two categories for Variable *B*?

20.4 Predicting categories

The same participants are tested on both variables. The reason for this is that the research hypothesis predicts that participants who are given a hint will be able to solve a problem. In order to test this hypothesis it is essential that the same participants are given a hint and then given the problem to solve. This makes it possible for the researcher to make predictions about the relationships between the two variables.

On the other hand, the pairs of conditions for each variable are defined independently. It is impossible for the same participants to be given a hint as well as not being given a hint. Equally, no one participant can simultaneously be in the category of being able to solve the problem and also in the category of not being able to solve the problem.

An example might be that a researcher predicts that participants who are in the category of being given favourable instructions about helping strangers are more likely to be in the category of helping an old lady across a road. Participants who are in the category of being warned about helping strangers are more likely to end up in the category of not helping a stranger.

There is one other special feature that arises from predicting the number of participants in different categories. In a typical experiment the experimenter selects the experimental conditions and decides how many participants will be used for each of the conditions.

The crucial distinction is that in a chi-square design the prediction is formulated as the number of participants who will turn out to be in each category. Rather than being a prior decision of the researcher, the predicted numbers of participants in each category cannot be known until the research is carried out.

In order to ensure that there will be a reasonable number of participants in each category, it is usual to recommend that quite a lot of participants are used for chi-square. Otherwise it might turn out that, in spite of the instructions, very few participants are prepared to help other people.

20.5   Selecting a statistical test in the Decision Chart

Relationships between variables?
The answer to this question is 'Yes'.

Are participants allocated to nominal categories?
The answer is 'Yes'.

If you look up 'relationships between variables' and 'nominal categories' in the Decision Chart you will arrive at the chi-square test. This is the appropriate statistical test for testing categorical data.

Using the chi-square test

When to use

The chi-square test should be used when participants are allocated to categories and the data are nominal. Remember that the test only deals with categories, not scores.

Research hypothesis

The researcher predicted that a higher proportion of technology students would use regular study patterns, as compared with social science students.

Sample data

A hundred participants are selected, one group of 50 social science students and another group of 50 technology students. A questionnaire was sent to all the students asking them to report whether their study patterns fall into one of three categories:

1 Regular day-to-day study.
2 Irregular bursts of study.
3 Mixture of both kinds of study.

There were 44 replies from social science and 42 replies from technology students. The replies about study patterns were allocated to the three categories. The results are shown in Table 20.1.

Table 20.1 Reported study patterns

	Study patterns			Totals of students
	Regular	Irregular	Mixed	
Group 1 (social science students)	Cell 1 6	Cell 2 15	Cell 3 23	44
Group 2 (technology students)	Cell 4 10	Cell 5 8	Cell 6 24	42
Totals for study patterns	16	23	47	86 Total number of participants (N)

Notes on Table 20.1

1 The table shows how many students are allocated to the three categories of study patterns.
2 The three study patterns are shown on the top line.
3 The two groups of social science and technology students are shown on the left-hand side of the table.
4 There are six cells in the table for two groups of students and three study patterns (2×3). These six cells are labelled cell 1, cell 2, etc.
5 In each cell the number of students in each category is indicated. In cell 1, 6 social science students reported regular study patterns; in cell 2, 15 social science students reported irregular study patterns; in cell 4, 10 technology students reported regular study patterns; in cell 6, 24 technology students reported mixed study patterns.
6 These numbers are known as observed frequencies because the number in each cell represents the frequency with which the students fall into the three study pattern categories.
7 The totals for the three study patterns are shown at the bottom of the table and the totals for the two groups of students on the right-hand side.
8 The grand total for all participants is 86, representing the 44 social science students plus the 42 technology students, and the totals for the study patterns.

? Question 20.2 (a) How many social science students reported mixed study patterns in cell 3?

(b) How many technology students reported irregular study patterns in cell 5?

(c) What was the total for regular study patterns?

(d) What was the total for mixed study patterns?

(e) What was the total of technology students?

Rationale

Table 20.1 gives the observed frequencies of the two categories of students who reported three categories of study patterns. These observed frequencies have to be compared with expected frequencies. Expected frequencies are calculated as if there were no bias towards a relationship between the two sets of categories. The expected frequencies represent the null hypothesis.

The expected frequencies have to be calculated taking into account the relevant totals. These totals reflect the proportions of the 44 social science and 42 technology students who would be expected to be in the three study pattern categories if it were equally probable that all students would be found in all categories.

The observed frequencies in Table 20.1 are compared with the null hypothesis of expected frequencies. If the observed frequencies are significantly different from the expected frequencies, the null hypothesis can be rejected.

Step-by-step instructions for calculating chi-square

These are given in Box L.

 Box L

Step-by-step instructions for calculating the value of χ^2

1 Note the *observed frequencies* (*O*) in cells 1–6 in Table 20.1.

Cell 1: $O = 6$
Cell 2: $O = 15$
Cell 3: $O = 23$
Cell 4: $O = 10$
Cell 5: $O = 8$
Cell 6: $O = 24$

2 Calculate the *expected frequencies* (*E*) for cells 1–6 in Table 20.1 by multiplying the two relevant marginal totals for each cell and dividing by the total number of participants (*N* = 86).

Cell 1: $E = \dfrac{16 \times 44}{86} = 8.19$

Cell 2: $E = \dfrac{23 \times 44}{86} = 11.77$

Cell 3: $E = \dfrac{47 \times 44}{86} = 24.05$

Cell 4: $E = \dfrac{16 \times 42}{86} = 7.81$

Cell 5: $E = \dfrac{23 \times 42}{86} = 11.23$

Cell 6: $E = \dfrac{47 \times 42}{86} = 22.95$

3 Calculate the value of χ^2 using the formula

$$\chi^2 = \Sigma \frac{(O - E)^2}{E}$$

Remember that squares of minus differences result in positive numbers.

$$= \frac{(6 - 8.19)^2}{8.19} + \frac{(15 - 11.77)^2}{11.77} + \frac{(23 - 24.05)^2}{24.05}$$
$$+ \frac{(10 - 7.81)^2}{7.81} + \frac{(8 - 11.23)^2}{11.23} + \frac{(24 - 22.95)^2}{22.95}$$

$= 0.58 \text{ (cell 1)} + 0.89 \text{ (cell 2)} + 0.05 \text{ (cell 3)}$
$+ 0.61 \text{ (cell 4)} + 0.93 \text{ (cell 5)} + 0.05 \text{ (cell 6)}$
$= 3.11$

4 Calculate the degrees of freedom:
    c = number of columns
    r = number of rows
    $df = (c - 1)(r - 1)$

$c = 3$
$r = 2$
$df = (3 - 1) \times (2 - 1) = 2$

Notes on calculations in Box L

1 The observed frequencies in each cell are taken from the cells in Table 20.1.
2 In order to calculate expected frequencies relevant totals have to be identified in the table. The relevant totals are as follows: cell 1 shows the 6 social science students who have regular study patterns. The relevant totals for cell 1 are the 44 social science students and the 16 regular study patterns reported by both types of students. For cell 5 the relevant totals are the total of 42 technology students and the total of 23 students who reported irregular study patterns. Once the relevant totals have been identified for each cell, the expected frequencies for each cell are calculated by multiplying these totals and dividing them by the grand total of 86 participants, as shown in Step 2.
3 The formula in step 3 calculates the sum of the squared differences between observed and expected frequencies.
4 The *df* are calculated as the three cells for study patterns minus 1 (3 − 1 = 2) and the two cells for types of students minus 1 (2 − 1 = 1). These are multiplied to produce *df* = 2.

? Question 20.3 What are the relevant totals for the following cells in Table 20.1?

(a) Cell 2

(b) Cell 3

(c) Cell 4

(d) Cell 6

Looking up the significance of chi-square in Table E

You have already used Table E for the Friedman test (related) in Chapter 11 and for the Kruskal–Wallis test (unrelated) in Chapter 12. In both these cases, chi-square in Table E was used when there were large numbers of participants.

The calculated value of chi-square has to be larger than the critical values in Table E. To look up chi-square look along the row for *df* = 2. The critical value for $p < 0.05$ is 5.99.

In Box L the calculated chi-square is 3.11. As this is smaller than the critical value of 5.99 the null hypothesis cannot be rejected. Another way of expressing this is that the observed frequencies were not significantly different from the expected frequencies.

Conclusions

The research hypothesis that more technology students would use regular study patterns as compared with social science students was not supported. The failure to find significant results can probably be explained by the large number of students who reported mixed study patterns, as shown in Table 20.1.

Chi-square can only test overall relationships between variables, which is equivalent to a two-tailed hypothesis. The reason for this is that it is possible to interpret relationships between variables in more than one way. For example, it is just as likely that students who have regular study patterns might decide to study technology, rather than that studying technology results in students learning good study habits.

 Progress box twenty

- Chi-square is based on predicted relationships between two variables represented as categories.
- Categories are identified for each variable.
- The measured data are nominal, which involves counting the number of participants in each of the categories.
- To calculate chi-square observed frequencies are compared with expected frequencies.

Pearson product moment correlation

21.1 Comparison with experiments

In all psychological research a researcher is testing a hypothesis about relationships between variables. The only issue is how much control researchers have over the variables in the design. Experimenters select independent variables and measure the dependent variable of participants' scores. The hypothesis predicts differences between scores.

The Pearson product moment correlation is a test of correlation. Predictions about correlations are quite different. In correlation the research hypothesis predicts that two variables will be associated with each other. Associations between variables are the basis for all correlations.

21.2 Measuring variables in correlations

The essential characteristic of correlational designs is that both variables are represented as continuous ranges of scores. The measures of participants' performance on both variables produce a range of scores.

An example would be if children were given a spelling test and a reading test. The measure of spelling would be a range of spelling scores produced by the children and the measure of reading scores would be a range of reading scores produced by the children.

The spelling scores would represent one variable and the reading scores a second variable. It is important to note that in correlational designs the same participants produce scores on both variables. This makes it possible for the researcher to make predictions about relationships between scores on both variables.

The fact that both variables are continuous has advantages. In experiments it is necessary to manipulate, groups of good and less good spellers and groups of good and less good readers. The advantage of a correlational design is that the full range of spelling scores can be compared with the full range of reading scores.

Because the two variables in a correlation design are represented by continuous ranges of scores, these count as interval data. Numerical calculations of sums of squares are required for the parametric Pearson correlation test.

21.3 Predicting positive correlations

The researcher predicts a relationship between the two variables, in our example children's scores on spelling and reading. The prediction might be that over the whole range of spelling ability and reading ability children who are good spellers will also tend to score highly on a reading test, while children at the bottom end of the spelling scale will not do so well at reading.

In this case it is predicted that the scores on the two variables will be positively related. This means that children who have high spelling scores will also have high reading scores. Likewise, low spelling scores are predicted to be associated with low reading scores.

Because the variables move in the same direction, this is known as a *positive* correlation. High scores on spelling 'go together' with high scores on reading, medium scores go with medium scores and low scores go with low scores.

? Question 21.1 Which of the following are most likely to result in a high positive correlation? Which are not likely to be correlated at all?

(a) Height and shoe size.

(b) Number of cinema tickets sold and the number of customers in the audience.

(c) Amount of spinach eaten and wins on football pools.

It is obvious from the examples in Question 21.1 that in some cases positive correlations between pairs of scores are likely to be high. Relationships between other pairs of scores are likely to produce a much lower amount of correlation, or no correlation at all. Another way of putting this is that some correlations are very high, while others are low or non-existent.

21.4   Predicting negative correlations

So far we have been talking about the amount of positive correlation between pairs of scores, like spelling and reading scores. But what about cases when high scores on one variable might be expected to be associated with low scores on another variable? For instance, children who achieve excellent scores on a quiz about sports may score low on writing essays, and vice versa.

It is important to realize that, if high scores on one variable are associated with low scores on another variable, this is still a correlation, but it is in the opposite direction to a positive correlation. This is known as a *negative* correlation because the scores on one variable are moving in the opposite direction to scores on the other variable.

In our example it is predicted that high scores on the sport quiz will be associated with low scores on essay writing. This is a negative correlation between high scores on one variable and low scores on the other variable.

? Question 21.2 Which of the following are likely to be positive correlations or negative correlations?

(a) Temperatures in winter and size of electricity bills.

(b) Amount of rain and sale of umbrellas.

21.5   Correlation coefficients

The next question is how to measure precisely the amount of correlation between two variables.

Correlations are measured in terms of correlation coefficients, which indicate the size of a correlation between two variables. Correlation coefficients run from zero, i.e. no correlation, to +1 for a perfect positive correlation. A perfect negative correlation is represented by −1.

In psychological research it is unlikely that any scores would be so perfectly correlated. Because of the infinite variability of human beings, there are sure to be some good spellers who are bad at reading. For this reason, most correlations between psychological variables are not perfectly correlated. Most correlations fall somewhere between the extremes of +1 (positive), −1 (negative) and zero (none).

? Question 21.3 (a) Which of the three correlation coefficients listed below expresses the lowest and the highest correlations? List them in order from lowest to highest.

+0.5   0   −0.9

(b) Which of these correlation coefficients is most likely to express the relationship between number of miles travelled and the cost of a second-class ticket?

(c) Which of these correlation coefficients is most likely to express the relationship between the number of pedestrian crossings in a town and average earnings?

(d) Which of these correlation coefficients is most likely to express the relationship between the amount of time spent practising the piano and the number of football games played?

To sum up, a correlation coefficient of zero means that there is no relation at all between the variables. The higher the correlation coefficient, whether positive or negative, the higher the correlation. Smaller correlation coefficients (such as +0.2 and −0.2) indicate lower correlations between variables.

21.6   Selecting a statistical test in the Decision Chart

Relationships between variables?
The answer to this question is 'Yes'.

Is it predicted that two variables are correlated?
The answer is 'Yes'.

If you look up 'relationships between variables' and 'correlations' in the Decision Chart you will arrive at the Pearson correlation. This is the appropriate statistical test for testing correlations between two variables.

21.7   Using Pearson correlation product moment correlation

When to use

The Pearson product moment correlation should be used when scores are correlated and the data are interval.

Research hypothesis

The prediction is that high arithmetic scores will be positively correlated with high reading scores. This is a one-tailed hypothesis predicting a positive correlation between the reading and arithmetic varibles.

? Question 21.4 Suppose a researcher predicted that there would either be a positive or a negative correlation between two sets of measured scores. Would this be a one-tailed or a two-tailed hypothesis?

Sample data

An arithmetic test and a reading test were administered to 12 children. The arithmetic scores (Variable *A*) and the reading scores (Variable *B*) are shown in Table 21.1.

Table 21.1   Scores on an arithmetic test and a reading test for 12 children

Parti-cipants	Variable A (arithmetic scores)	Variable B (reading scores)	$a \times b$	a^2	b^2
1	32	17	544	1 024	289
2	54	13	702	2 916	169
3	68	14	952	4 624	196
4	93	10	930	8 649	100
5	87	16	1392	7 569	256
6	24	7	168	576	49
7	49	6	294	2 401	36
8	35	18	630	1 225	324
9	97	19	1843	9 409	361
10	62	13	806	3 844	169
11	44	9	396	1 936	81
12	73	12	876	5 329	144

Total $\Sigma a = 718$ $\Sigma b = 154$ $\Sigma(a \times b) = 9533$ $\Sigma a^2 = 49\ 502$ $\Sigma b^2 = 2174$

Notes on Table 21.1
1 The arithmetic and reading scores are shown for each of the 12 participants.
2 The sums are shown for the scores on both variables.

3 In the third column each of the a scores is multiplied by each of the b scores ($a \times b$) and the sum of these is calculated. This represents the predicted variance between the A and B variables.

4 In the a^2 column each a score is squared and summed and in the b^2 column each b score is squared and summed. These summed squares represent the total variance.

Rationale

The aim of the Pearson correlation is to test whether scores on one variable are related to scores on the other variable. This is measured by whether a correlation coefficient is high enough to be significant. It is important to note that a correlation has to be reasonably high to be considered as being possibly significant. If a researcher is investigating a very large number of subjects, a quite low correlation might turn out to be significant. For this reason, it is usually accepted that there should be a reasonably high correlation, say 0.5 or better, before carrying out a test to assess its significance.

The correlation is a ratio between the predicted variance in scores and the total variance in scores. If the ratio is low, the null hypothesis cannot be rejected. The ratio is denoted by r.

Step-by step instructions for calculating r

These are given in Box M.

 Box M

Step-by-Step Instructions for Calculating the Value of r

1   For each participant multiply the A variable score by the B variable score   See $a \times b$ column in Table 21.1.

2   Square individual scores for Variable A and for Variable B See a^2 and b^2 columns in Table 21.1

3   Calculate

     N = number of participants $N = 12$

     $\Sigma a \times b$ = total of $a \times b$ column $\Sigma a \times b = 9533$

     Σa and Σb = totals for each variable $\Sigma a = 718$

                                                   $\Sigma b = 154$

$(\Sigma a)^2$ and $(\Sigma b)^2$ = totals for each variable squared $(\Sigma a)^2 = 718^2$
$(\Sigma b)^2 = 154^2$

Σa^2 and Σb^2 = sums of squared individual scores $\Sigma a^2 = 49\,502$
$\Sigma b^2 = 2174$

4   Find the value of r from the formula

$$r = \frac{N\Sigma a \times b - \Sigma a \times \Sigma b}{\sqrt{[N\Sigma a^2 - (\Sigma a)^2][N\Sigma b^2 - (\Sigma b)^2]}}$$

$$= \frac{(12 \times 9533) - (718 \times 154)}{\sqrt{(12 \times 49\,502 - 718^2)(12 \times 2174 - 154^2)}}$$

$$= \frac{114\,396 - 110\,572}{\sqrt{(594\,024 - 515\,524)(26\,088 - 23\,716)}}$$

$$= \frac{3824}{\sqrt{78\,500 \times 2372}}$$

$$= \frac{3824}{\sqrt{186\,202\,000}}$$

$$= \frac{3824}{13\,645.5}$$

$$= 0.28$$

5   Calculate df, i.e. number of participants minus 2 $df = N - 2 = 12 - 2 = 10$

Notes on the calculations in Box M

1   Steps 1, 2 and 3 refer back to the calculations carried out in Table 21.1.

2   The formula in step 4 gives the calculation of the predicted variance on the top line of the formula.

3   The sums of squares on the bottom line of the formula give the variance for the *A* variable multiplied by the variance for the *B* variable. These two variances represent total variance. Note that the square root has to be taken of the total variance.

4   The total formula in Step 4 represents the ratio between the predicted variance and total variance.

5   In step 5 the *df* are defined as number of participants minus 1 for Variable A and number of participants minus 1 for Variable B. This amounts to total number of participants minus 2 (in our example $12 - 2 = 10\ df$).

Looking up the significance of *r* in Table H

The calculated *r* in Box M of 0.28 is a pretty low correlation. Normally, it would be assumed that the correlation is not significantly different from a zero correlation and so the null hypothesis cannot be rejected.

However, the sample of twelve participants was very small to test a correlation. In order to demonstrate how to look up *r* in Table H we will assume that there were 50 participants. Table H gives the critical values for different levels of significance levels for one-tailed and two-tailed hypotheses. The calculated *r* has to be equal to or larger than the critical values. You first need to identify the degrees of freedom (in our new example *df* = 50). If you look along the row for 50 *df* for a one-tailed significance level ($p < 0.05$) the critical value is 0.2306. The calculated *r* of 0.28 is higher than this value and so the null hypothesis can be rejected.

Conclusions

The *r* of 0.28 was too low to be significant. The research hypothesis that there would be a positive correlation between arithmetic and reading scores was not supported.

Note that, even if the value of *r* had been significant, there are usually several possible explanations for a relationship between variables. It is not always possible to identify the precise reason for the relationship.

Possible explanations for a relationship between two variables of reading scores and spelling scores are shown below:

1 Spelling ability may be responsible for improving reading.
2 Being a good reader improves spelling.
3 Both good spelling and good reading are the result of some other variable altogether, such as a positive attitude by parents towards school lessons.

? Question 21.5 (a) What would be three possible explanations if a significant positive correlation was found between arithmetic and reading? *Hint*: look at the example of three explanations for spelling and reading above.

(b) What would be a likely explanation for a correlation between a cock crowing and an alarm clock going off?

In some cases it may be likely that a correlation represents a causal explanation. The strong and consistent correlation between smoking and lung cancer has led to acceptance of a causal connection. But, in principle, it is possible that there is some other common factor affecting the use of cigarettes and a predisposition to lung cancer. That is why medical research has been undertaken to discover physiological mechanisms in order to indicate a direct causal link.

 Progress box twenty one

- Correlation represents a predicted relationship between two variables.
- Correlations are measured on a scale running from +1 (perfect positive correlation) to 0 (no correlation) to −1 (perfect negative correlation).
- A reasonably high correlation (0.5) is required before testing the significance of a correlation.

22 Introduction to simple linear regression

22.1 Comparisons with correlation

The type of linear regression discussed in this chapter is called *simple* regression. In simple linear regression only two variables are tested, as in correlation. This is to distinguish it from multiple regression, which will be described in Chapter 23.

There are quite a few similarities between correlation and simple linear regression. The main point that they have in common is that they are both concerned with relationships between two variables.

Another similarity is that the scores on both variables represent continuous scores. The scores for both variables are interval data.

We will show that both correlation and simple linear regression can be demonstrated using graphs that are called scatterplots. We will also see that error is measured in a very similar way for both types of analysis.

The big difference is the aim of the researcher. In Chapter 21 we set out to show how two sets of scores are correlated with each other. For example, both spelling scores and reading scores are measured and the correlation between then is calculated. The researcher is simply interested in whether a correlation is found between the two variables. In linear regression, by contrast, the scores on the two variables are not treated as correlated. Instead the scores on one variable are used to predict scores on the other variable.

An example would be if children's reading scores are used to predict their arithmetic scores. The assumption would be that, if the researcher knows children's reading scores it would be possible to predict their arithmetic scores.

22.2   Predictor variable and criterion variable

The variable that is selected to predict scores on the other variable is usually called a predictor variable. The other variable, on which scores are to be predicted, is often called the criterion variable.

It is usual to denote the scores on the predictor variable by the symbol X and the scores on the predicted criterion variable by the symbol Y. In our example the predictor variable X represents the reading scores, which are used to predict the variable Y arithmetic scores.

? Question 22.1   (a) Is Variable A (arithmetic scores) or Variable B (reading scores) the predictor variable?

(b) Which of these two variables is the criterion variable?

(c) Which of the scores on the two variables is represented by the symbol X and which by the symbol Y?

We will take as an example the scores for two variables given in Table 22.1. The aim of the researcher is to predict children's arithmetic scores on the basis of their reading scores.

Table 22.1   Arithmetic scores (Variable A) and reading scores (Variable B)

Child	Arithmetic score	Reading score
1	9	2
2	10	3
3	12	1
4	6	1
5	11	4
6	9	1
7	12	5
8	16	8
9	13	5
10	10	3
11	13	6
12	14	7

22.3 Scatterplots

Scatterplots can be drawn to show relationships between two variables. They are called scatterplots because dots representing scores on variables are plotted in graphs, enabling a 'scatter' to be seen.

Scatterplots can be used to represent a correlation between scores. As we shall see, they can also be used to show the relationship between the predictor variable and the predicted criterion variable.

The scatterplot for the arithmetic and reading scores in Table 22.1 is shown in Figure 22.1.

A scatterplot is a graph constructed by placing the criterion variable (arithmetic scores) up the vertical axis of the graph and predictor variable (reading scores) along the horizontal axis at the bottom of the graph.

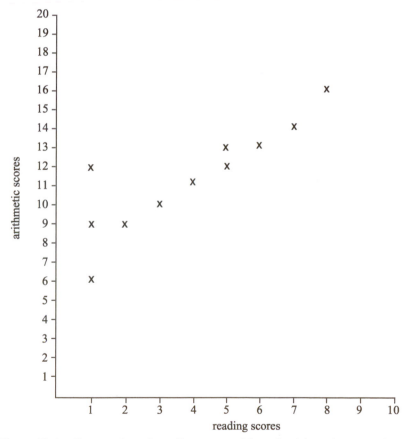

Figure 22.1   Scatterplot of reading scores (X) and arithmetic scores (Y) from Table 22.1.

Each child is allocated a dot in the scatterplot, which represents that child's scores for arithmetic and reading. For example, child 1 in Table 22.1 has an arithmetic score of 9 and a reading score of 2. These scores are plotted up the vertical axis as a score of 9 and along the bottom axis as a score of 2.

In order to locate this dot on the scatterplot look along the bottom line for a reading score of 2 and from the vertical axis for an arithmetic score of 9. Where these two scores meet is the dot for child 1. You will notice that there is only one dot for a reading score of 2 and that dot has an arithmetic score of 9. So this dot represents the reading and arithmetic scores for child 1.

? Question 22.2 Which child numbers are represented by the first three dots at the left-hand side of the scatterplot? *Hint*: look at the scores in Table 22.1.

The points plotted in the scatterplot in Figure 22.1 seem to show that there is a positive linear relationship between arithmetic scores and reading scores. If you look at the reading scores along the bottom line, high reading scores tend to predict high arithmetic scores and lower reading scores tend to predict lower arithmetic scores.

22.4   Regression equation for calculating a regression line

As we said earlier, in simple linear regression one of the two variables is a predictor variable, which is used to predict scores on the criterion variable. The predictor variable X (reading scores) is used to predict variable Y (arithmetic scores). The predicted Y scores are denoted by Y'.

The aim is to construct a line on the scatter plot which links up the predictor variable scores (X) and the predicted Y scores (Y'). This is called a regression line, and shows how the Y' scores are predicted by the X scores.

The regression equation defines the regression line. The regression equation is given by

$$Y' = A + BX.$$

A is the point at which Y' is calculated when the X variable is set to zero. It is called the intercept because it is where the regression line cuts the Y line in the absence of the X predictor variable.

The equation $Y' = A + BX$ is a mathematical expression for a straight line. This line is called the regression line because it represents the effect of the predictor X scores on the predicted Y' scores.

The slope of the regression line represents the degree to which the scores on Y' are predictable by the scores on the predictor variable X. This make it possible to read off the predicted scores for Y' for each score of X.

The reason for defining A is that it provides a baseline when the predictor X scores are zero. This is a technical concept. There is often no psychological meaning attached to considering what a child's arithmetic score would be if they had a nil reading score.

An example to indicate what a regression line connecting the dots in the scatterplot in Figure 22.1 could look like is shown in Figure 22.2.

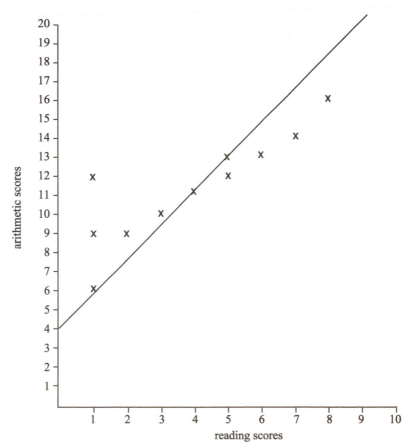

Figure 22.2 Regression line linking reading scores (X) and arithmetic scores (Y).

22.5 Residual error

The straight regression line in Figure 22.2 illustrates a linear relationship between the dots in the scatterplot representing predictor X reading scores and predicted Y' arithmetic scores.

The regression line can be thought of as an ideal condition in which all the predicted Y' scores should be the same as the arithmetic scores. The dots in the scatterplot represent the actual reading and arithmetic scores.

It is important to note that not all the dots representing scores are connected by the regression line. This is due to individual differences between participants. It would not be expected that all the children would have exactly the same range of arithmetic and reading scores.

For example, in Table 22.1 child 3 obtained a score of only 1 for reading but a score of 12 for arithmetic. This is the dot on the left-hand side of the scatterplot representing a score of 1 on reading and a score of 12 on arithmetic.

This particular example goes against the prediction that arithmetic scores can be predicted on the basis of reading scores. Looking at the low reading score for child 3, a low arithmetic score would have been predicted rather than a high score of 12.

The fact that the regression line does not connect all the dots means that there is error in the dots representing children's scores. Error is measured as the differences between the actual scores and the scores predicted by the regression line.

These differences can be thought of as deviations in scores from the predicted scores. These deviations are called *residual error*. All error is residual because error is what is left over after predicted variance has been accounted for.

Deviations from the regression line can be calculated as differences between predicted Y' scores and actual observed Y scores. The deviations between predicted and actual Y scores are measured as $Y - Y'$. These deviations represent residual error.

It is interesting to note that some of the dots are quite near the regression line. The aim is to solve the linear regression equation so as to result in the smallest deviations between predicted Y' scores and observed Y scores.

22.6 Rationale for using ANOVA as a test of linear regression

It may sometimes be useful to be able to read off Y scores on the basis of X scores in order to predict new cases of arithmetic scores. However, researchers are often more interested in whether regression lines represent a good prediction of the predicted Y' scores in relation to observed Y scores.

The deviations between predicted Y' scores and actual Y scores are measured by the sums of deviations squared. This is how sums of squares are calculated in ANOVA as deviations between the scores and the means.

So it should not come as too much of a surprise that ANOVA is the appropriate test for the significance of the predictions made on the basis of predictor variables.

ANOVA is used to test different sources of variance. In linear regression there are two sources of variance, which make up total variance.

1 Predicted variance in Y scores accounted for by the predicted Y' scores on the basis of the predictor variable X (predicted linear regression).
2 Residual error as a result of unpredicted differences in Y scores not explained by the predictor variable X (residual error variance).

Sums of squares are calculated for each source of variance. In the usual way these sums of squares are divided by the *df* to produce mean squares. The predicted mean square divided by the error mean square results in the F ratio.

If the ANOVA is not significant this implies that there is too much residual error reflecting deviations from the regression line. If all the dots are scattered randomly, as stated by the null hypothesis, it will be impossible to calculate a best-fit regression line to minimize deviations. In this case the null hypothesis cannot be rejected.

22.7   ANOVA table to test linear regression

An ANOVA table for simple linear regression is shown in Table 22.2.

Table 22.2   ANOVA table for linear regression

Source	df	Sum of squares	Mean squares	F ratio	Significance
Regression	1	57.49	57.49	27.69 (df 1,10)	$p < 0.0005$
Residual	10	20.76	2.08		
Total	11	78.25			

Notes on Table 22.2

1 The sources of variance are regression (predicted) and residual (error).
2 There were 12 participants so the total *df* is $12 - 1 = 11$. The *df* for regression is $df = 1$ because there is only one predictor variable. The *df* for error are the remaining *df* $11 - 1 = 10$.
3 The residual sum of squares is calculated by subtracting the regression sum of squares from total sum of squares.
4 A large amount of variance is accounted for by the predicted regression with a relatively small error.
5 This results in a highly significant *F* ratio.

Conclusions

The significance of ANOVA for linear regression demonstrates that reading scores are a good predictor of arithmetic scores.

It is important to note that this prediction is based on a relationship between variables. For example, it might be possible that the linear relationship between variables works in the opposite direction. It might turn out that it is easier to predict children's reading scores (*Y* variable) from knowing their arithmetic scores (predictor *X* variable).

 Progress box twenty two

- In linear regression the scores on a predictor variable (*X*) are used to predict scores on a criterion variable (*Y′*).
- Regression lines are calculated to minimize the deviations between the predicted *Y′* scores and the observed *Y* scores (residual error).
- Linear regression is tested by ANOVA with regression as the predicted variance and deviations as residual error.

23 Multiple regression

23.1 Comparison with simple regression

In Section 21.5 we described correlation coefficients as a measure of the correlational association between two variables. As explained in Section 22.1, the difference between correlation and regression is that in regression one of the variables is selected as a predictor variable, which predicts scores on the other variable.

Multiple regression introduces several predictor variables. For instance, there could be three predictor variables all predicting scores on the predicted criterion variable. Because the same participants produce scores on all four variables, it is possible to calculate relationships between all the variables.

As in Chapter 22, in our discussion of multiple regression we will be using the terminology of predictor variables and criterion variable. As with simple linear regression, the predictor variables are denoted X, in this case three predictor variables X_1, X_2 and X_3. The criterion variable is denoted Y.

The aim of multiple regression analysis is to investigate the extent to which the scores on the predictor X variables succeed in predicting scores on the Y variable.

23.2 Objectives of multiple regression

This section will give a brief introduction to some of the main features of multiple regression in order to prepare you for later discussions.

Objective 1

To assess the extent to which scores on predictor X variables are associated with Y scores.

One of the main methods to test this is to carry out multiple correlations between all the variables to assess the significance of correlation coefficients between all pairs of variables, each predictor with the predicted criterion variable and also between pairs of predicators. Multiple correlations are usually shown in the form of a multiple correlation matrix, as in Table 23.1.

Table 23.1   Sample multiple correlation matrix

	Y	X_1	X_2	X_3
Y	1	0.67	0.52	0.74
X_1	0.67	1	0.42	0.21
X_2	0.52	0.42	1	0.52
X_3	0.74	0.21	0.52	1

Notes on Table 23.1
1 Each of the figures in the table represents a correlation between each of the three predictors (X_1, X_2, X_3) and the predicted criterion variable (Y). The matrix also shows the correlation coefficients between the predictors themselves.
2 You should notice that the correlations between variables are given twice. For instance, the correlation between Y and X_1 of 0.67 is the same as the correlation between X_1 and Y of 0.67.
3 The correlation of a variable with itself, e.g. Y and Y, is always 1.

? Question 23.1

(a) What is the correlation between Y and X_2?

(b) What is the correlation between X_2 and X_2?

It is important to realize that the most desirable outcome is to find significant correlations between the scores on the predictor X variables and the scores on the criterion Y variable.

In Table 23.1 the correlations between the three X variables and the Y variable are all high (0.67, 0.52, 0.74). These correlations between the predictor X variables and the Y criterion variable would be good evidence that the scores on the predictor X variables have a significant effect on the scores on the Y variable.

The correlations in the matrix can be thought of as individual correlations, each of which could be tested by the Pearson correlation test of r. To express the effect of all the correlations together the term multiple R is used.

Objective 2

To assess the significance of the variance on the predicted criterion variable contributed by all the predictor variables simultaneously.

It is possible to calculate the square of multiple R, called R^2 or R-square. R^2 is very important because it is a measure of the predicted multiple regression that can be explained by the predictor variables. This is expressed as the amount of total variance in Y scores accounted for by the predictor X variables.

The next step is to assess the significance of the predicted variance. The way in which the regression variance is tested is to compare it with error variance. This results in a ratio between predicted regression variance and error variance.

The idea of a ratio between two sources of variance, consisting of predicted variance and error variance, should remind you of Chapters 14 and 15, which described ANOVA in just these terms. It is not surprising, then, that ANOVA is used to test R^2 as a measure of predicted regression variance. An outline ANOVA table showing the sources of variance is shown in Table 23.2

Table 23.2 Outline ANOVA table

Sources of variance	Sum of Squares	df	Mean Square	F	Sig.
Regression					
Residual					
Total					

Notes on Table 23.2
1 Under the first column, sources of variance, the line for regression variance represents the proportion of predicted variance (measured by R^2) contributed by the predictor X variables.

2 Residual represents the proportion of error variance in Y scores that is not accounted for by the predictor variables. This is called residual error because, as with all error, it represents what is 'left over' after all the predicted variance has been accounted for.

3 Residual error can be defined formally as deviations between the predicted Y' scores and the actual observed Y scores ($Y - Y'$), as discussed in Section 22.5. In practice, residual error is calculated by subtracting predicted regression variance from total variance, as is usual in ANOVA tables.

Objective 3

To assess the predictive effects of individual X predictor variables.

So far we have considered the effects of the variance in Y scores accounted for by all X predictor variables.

It is also important to estimate the contribution of each X predictor variable in predicting the Y scores. In order to compare the effects of individual predictors we need to standardize each predictor variable so that they can be compared on an identical scale. These standardized versions of the B coefficients for each predictor variable are known as beta values. Betas will be described in a later section.

As you will remember from Chapters 9 and 10, t tests are designed to test comparisons between pairs of conditions. This is why t tests are particularly suitable for making individual comparisons between coefficients for each predictor variable and the error associated with each one.

23.3 Types of multiple regression

There are three main types of multiple regression analysis, namely, *standard* multiple regression, *sequential* multiple regression and *statistical* multiple regression. The last two types were evolved to meet specific problems related to the order in which each predictor variable enters the multiple regression analysis.

We need to assess which type of multiple regression should be used after inspection of the data. It is usual to start with standard multiple regression.

Standard multiple regression

In standard multiple regression all predictors are entered simultaneously into the multiple regression. This allows the effect of each predictor variable to be compared with the effects of all the other predictor variables at the same time.

Technically, so that each predictor variable can be tested against all the other predictor variables, each predictor variable is treated 'as if' it has been entered last into the analysis. The point of this 'as if' condition is that each variable will be analysed in relation to all the variables that have already been entered. This meets the requirement that each predictor variable is compared with all the previously entered variables.

What standard multiple regression analysis does is to determine the effect of all predictor variables in contributing to total variance, i.e. the proportion of variance that can be attributed to all the predictor variables.

As its name implies, standard multiple regression should always be used as a norm.

Sequential multiple regression

In standard multiple regression the predictor variables are entered so as to ensure that all variables are analysed against all the other variables. But sometimes the researcher may want to decide on a particular order of the predictor variables being entered into the multiple regression.

This can be achieved by using sequential multiple regression. Note that sequential regression is sometimes called *hierarchical* regression because it determines the hierarchical order in which variables are entered into the multiple regression.

In this type of multiple regression the researcher determines the order in which each predictor variable enters the analysis. The effect of each predictor variable in contributing to predicted variance is assessed separately at its point of entry. This contrasts with standard multiple regression, which analyses the combined effect of all the predictor variables.

The researcher determines the order of entry of each predictor variable on the grounds of theoretical evidence about the relative weight of each single variable. The researcher gives priority to variables that have been shown to have a significant effect on predicted performance.

One problem is that researchers might favour certain variables as opposed to other variables that could have an equal effect. In order to control for this possibility of bias, researchers are recommended to select an order of entry in which less favoured predictor variables are entered into the analysis before the theoretically based predictor variables. If the theoretical predictors are still found to have an effect, this is good evidence in support of these selected variables.

Statistical multiple regression

There are various sub-types of statistical multiple regression. The order of entry of the predictors is based purely on statistical grounds, leading often to grave problems of interpretation of results. All types of statistical regression should only be applied to very large samples when a researcher wants to find a subset of predictors that explain a large proportion of predicted variance.

Statistical multiple regression is a controversial, and somewhat advanced, technique that should be applied with great care in special circumstances.

23.4   Selecting a statistical test in the Decision Chart

Relationships between variables?
The answer to this question is 'Yes'.

Are *Y* scores predicted by *X* scores on predictor variables?
The answer is 'Yes'.

If you look up 'relationships between variables' and 'predictor variables' you will arrive at multiple regression. This consists of procedures for analysing regression for a set of multiple predictors.

23.5   Using multiple regression

When to use

Multiple regression is used when we want to predict effects of several predictor variables on a criterion variable. Predictor variables may be measured on a continuous scale or be categorical. An example of a categorical variable would be a predictor variable that noted whether children had attended a nursery school or not attended a nursery school. This is called a categorical variable because there are only two outcomes, attendance or not attendance.

Note that the criterion variable must always be a continuous variable.

Research hypothesis

It is predicted that three predictor variables, peer interaction, child–teacher interaction and supervision of daily activities, will affect scores on the criterion variable of group involvement.

Sample data

In the example, group involvement (GI) is the predicted criterion variable
Y and peer interaction (PI), child–teacher interaction (CTI) and supervision of daily activities (SDA) are the three predictor variables. All
three predictor variables when tested independently by other researchers
were found to be significantly correlated with group involvement. Thirty
children attending a crèche and their teachers were the participants in this
study.

Researchers carrying out the study used observational techniques to col-
lect data on the four variables. You will notice from the scores in Table 23.3

Table 23.3 Table of scores

Children	GI	PI	CTI	SDA
1	81.11	3	2	2
2	94.00	4	4	4
3	85.20	5	7	5
4	95.57	6	7	7
5	81.40	3	3	2
6	87.50	4	2	3
7	76.61	6	4	2
8	82.60	2	2	1
9	83.13	3	4	4
10	90.21	4	4	4
11	85.00	4	2	3
12	93.10	4	4	2
13	81.25	5	2	2
14	83.55	4	2	2
15	88.50	3	2	1
16	84.37	3	1	2
17	91.12	6	6	4
18	84.60	4	4	4
19	85.72	4	4	4
20	91.62	7	4	6
21	74.93	3	3	2
22	85.52	4	4	2
23	88.53	5	7	2
24	92.19	6	6	7
25	82.38	6	6	4
26	89.00	3	3	2
27	88.66	4	1	4
28	87.84	3	2	2
29	88.59	4	6	1
30	89.61	4	4	4

that the scores on the variables were measured on different rating scales. For example GI scores are expressed with decimal points and all appear to be very high in comparison with the scores obtained for the other three variables. This demonstrates that researchers often use different rating scales for measuring variables. All observational sessions were video-taped so that independent judges could validate the scores originally allocated by the researchers.

Rationale

The rationale for multiple regression is twofold. In the first place it is necessary to determine whether the regression variance, i.e. the variance accounted for by the effect of the predictor variables on the predicted criterion variable, is significantly higher than the variance due to the effect of residual error. As explained in Section 23.2 (Objective 2), regression variance is tested by ANOVA.

Secondly, it is necessary to determine the relative weight of each of the individual predictors on the predicted criterion variable scores. As explained in Section 23.2 (Objective 3), regression analysis performs a series of t tests between each predictor and its own error to test the significance of individual predictor variables.

If the residual variance is high, as predicted by the null hypothesis, the null hypothesis cannot be rejected.

Step-by-step instructions for interpreting multiple regression

These are given in Box N.

Note There are no calculations in this box and the tables. The aim is to understand computer printouts of multiple regression data.

 Box N

Step-by-step instructions for multiple regression equation

The equation for calculating regression lines in multiple regression is

$$Y' = A + B_1X_1 + B_2X_2 + B_3X_3$$

Y' predicted scores on the criterion variable of group involvement (GI)

A the intercept, representing the score on Y' when the three X variables are zero

B_1X_1 the regression coefficient for the slope of the regression line for the predictor variable PI multiplied by values of PI

B_2X_2 the regression coefficient for the slope of the regression line for the predictor variable CTI multiplied by values of CTI

B_3X_3 the regression coefficient for the slope of the regression line of the predictor variable SDA multiplied by values of SDA.

Notes on regression equation

1 The multiple regression equation is a mathematical expression for straight lines representing the slopes of the regression lines.

2 As in the simple equation, Y' equals predicted Y scores on the criterion variable GI.

3 In multiple regression A represents a common intercept for all three predictor variables. A is also known as the constant, because it is the same for all three predictor variables.

4 In the multiple regression equation there are several BX coefficients. These are known as B coefficients. The regression equation for multiple regression predicts Y scores by calculating regression lines for each of the three predictor variables.

5 The next tables interpret the outputs of a simplified SPSS computer analysis of multiple regression. Table 23.4 shows the output of the SPSS program in the form of descriptive statistics. It gives the means, the standard deviations and the number of participants for the predicted criterion variable (GI) and the three predictor variables (PI, CTI and SDA).

6 Table 23.5 shows the correlations between variables in the form of a multiple correlation matrix. It also gives the significance of each correlation.

Table 23.4 Descriptive statistics

	Mean	*Std. Deviation*	*N*
GI	86.4468	4.88375	30
PI	4.20	1.215	30
CTI	3.73	1.799	30
SDA	3.13	1.634	30

Table 23.5 Multiple correlation matrix

		GI	PI	CTI	SDA
Correlation	GI	1.000	0.299	0.349	0.490
	PI	0.299	1.000	0.625	0.646
	CTI	0.349	0.625	1.000	0.505
	SDA	0.490	0.646	0.505	1.000
Sig. (1-tailed)	GI		0.054	0.029	0.003
	PI	0.054		0.000	0.000
	CTI	0.029	0.000		0.002
	SDA	0.003	0.000	0.002	

Notes on Table 23.5
1 The multiple correlation matrix is in the same form as that shown in Table 23.1.
2 Correlation coefficients are shown between the variables including the predicted criterion variable (GI) and the three predictor variables (PI, CTI and SDA).
3 Using the Pearson product moment correlation (see Chapter 21), significance can be calculated for each correlation.

Looking at the correlations in Table 23.5, there are significant correlations between the predictor variables CTI and SDA with the criterion variable (GI). But the correlation between PI and GI is just above the conventional $p < 0.05$ and so is not significant.

There are also some significant correlations between predictor variables, between SDA and PI and SDA and CTI. Significant correlations between predictor variables can indicate that scores on one predictor variable are highly associated with scores on another predictor variable. For example, family income and choice of private schools might be so highly correlated that they do not add anything extra to the analysis. It can be argued that there is no need to investigate income if this also determines parents' choice of schools.

In Table 23.5 there may seem to be quite high significant correlations between predictor variables. It is important to note that, if there were very high correlations between a pair of predictor variables, the computer program itself would automatically throw out one of the paired variables. As none of the correlations between predictor variables have been identified as being too high, all the predictor variables are retained in the multiple regression for further analysis.

The data in Table 23.6 give the values of several important measures required for multiple regression.

Table 23.6 Calculation of multiple R and R^2

Multiple R	0.511
R^2	0.261
Adjusted R^2	0.176
Std. error	4.43409

Notes on Table 23.6

1 Multiple R represents a summary of all the correlations in the multiple correlation matrix.

2 R^2 represents the proportion of variance contributed by the predictor variables.

3 Adjusted R^2 is calculated taking into count the number of predictors. It should be used when many predictor variables are included in the regression. It is a corrective measure because, when many predictors are added to the regression, R^2 can become artificially high just by chance.

The next step in the multiple regression analysis involves finding out whether the variance accounted for by the three predictors on the predicted criterion variable is significant when compared to the effect of residual error.

The value of the constant A has to be tested as one of the predictors that may affect Y scores.

In Section 23.2 (Objective 2), the use of ANOVA was introduced as a test of the proportion of variance accounted for by the regression coefficients calculated for each predictor variable, including the A constant.

The ANOVA table shown in Table 23.7 is based on the data for 30 children in Table 23.3.

Table 23.7 ANOVA test of predictor variables

	Sum of Squares	*df*	*Mean Square*	*F*	*Sig.*
Regression	180.489	3	60.163	3.060	0.046
Residual	511.190	26	19.661		
Total	691.679	29			

Notes on Table 23.7

1 Regression variance is based on the proportion of variance in Y scores accounted for by all the predictor variables, including A, as measured by R^2.

2 Residual variance represents the error in Y scores that is not accounted for by predictor variables.

3 Total variance represents all the variance in *Y* scores.

4 Residual error is calculated by subtracting predicted regression variance from total variance.

5 The total *df* are calculated as $30 - 1 = 29$. Three df are allocated to the three predictor variables. The *df* for residual error are the remaining $df = 26$.

6 The *F* ratio is calculated in the usual way.

7 Looking up Table G(1) for ANOVA, the critical value of *F* for df 3, 26 is 2.98. The calculated *F* of 3.06 is larger than the critical value so the null hypothesis can be rejected ($p < 0.05$). In Table 23.7 there is an equivalent significance level of 0.046.

8 The conclusion is that the predicted regression variance accounted for by the predictor variables is supported by the data.

The last step in the multiple regression analysis is to calculate the relative weights of each individual predictor variable in predicting scores on the criterion *Y* variable. The terms relevant to this objective are shown in Table 23.8.

Table 23.8 Tests for relative weights of individual variables on G1

	Unstandardized coefficients		Standardized coefficients		
	B	Std. Error	Beta	t	Sig.
(Constant)	82.216	2.979		27.596	0.000
PI	−0.506	0.996	−0.126	−0.508	0.616
CTI	0.507	0.595	0.187	0.852	0.402
SDA	1.424	0.670	0.477	2.126	0.043

Notes on Table 23.8

1 The first column of *B* coefficients are the same *B* coefficients describing the slope of each regression line, plus the constant shown in our regression equation above.

2 The standard error in the next column is a measure of the error for the *B* coefficients for each predictor variable.

3 The final column indicates the *t* values found for the constant and the three predictor variables, i.e. the comparisons between the *B*s and their associated error terms.

4 The standardized beta coefficient for each predictor variable gives the relative weight of each predictor variable on the unit of change in the criterion *Y* variable.

Using the data in Table 23.8, the method for calculating the relative weight of each predictor variable is to standardize the *B* coefficients so that they can be compared on an identical scale. The standardized *B* coefficients are called beta coefficients. Because betas are standardized, beta coefficients allow us to test the relative contribution of each predictor variable in terms of a unit change in the scores of the criterion variable. Using these standardized beta coefficients, each predictor variable can be compared in terms of how much it contributes to units of change in the criterion variable compared with other variables.

The method for comparing individual predictor variables is to test the contribution of each variable to the total variance in *Y* scores. You will see in Table 23.8 that, for each of the *B* coefficients and the constant, a standard error is given.

As explained in Section 23.2 (Objective 3), *t* tests are used to test the significance of coefficients against their own error. In this case each B coefficient is tested against the appropriate standard error. The ratio for the *t* test is the *B* coefficient over its own standard error. Looking at the significance of the *t* tests the only individual predictor variable that was significant was SDA.

The other variable that was very significant was the constant. You will remember that the constant is *A*, which is the intercept for the regression lines for all the predictor variables. The importance of the constant is that it ensures that the same point of intersection holds for the population from which the children's scores are drawn.

Conclusions

The multiple regression matrix in Table 23.5 shows the significant correlations between the four variables, GI (the predicted criterion variable) and PI, CTI and SDA (the predictors). PI was not significantly correlated with the predicted criterion variable, making doubtful its contribution to scores on GI. Correlations of the other two predictors with GI were significant, as were some of the correlations between predictors. None of the correlations between predictor variables was identified as being too high. So all the predictor variables were retained in the multiple regression analysis. (It was earlier noted that when correlations between predictor variables are too high the computer program automatically excludes one of the variables.)

Multiple *R* was 0.511. R^2 was calculated as 0.261, representing the predicted proportion of variance, and adjusted R^2 was 0.176. The ANOVA to assess the regression effects of all three predictor variables was significant ($p < 0.05$). The *t* tests to test the significance of the *B* coefficients associated with each of the predictor variables confirmed that the only predictor with a significant contribution to the variance on the criterion variable is SDA. This would indicate that the correlation coefficient for SDA accounted for most of the differences in *Y* scores. This was borne out by the high correlation between SDA and GI in the correlation matrix in Table 23.5.

The interpretation of these results shows that supervision of daily activities had a significant effect on the selected criterion variable of group involvement. Contrary to other findings, group involvement and peer interaction were not significantly correlated. On the other hand, child–teacher interaction and supervision of daily activities, as predicted by other studies, were significantly correlated with group involvement. The important point to make is that by means of regression we were able to determine that, when these two predictors are compared simultaneously, only one of them (SDA) appears to contribute significantly to the variance on the predicted criterion variable GI.

Why is peer interaction not correlated with group involvement? Group involvement measures the extent to which children get involved in a task set by the teacher and cooperate among themselves to get it done. The amount of peer interaction among them may not influence directly their involvement in the task, as is borne out by the low correlation between PI and GI. Other variables may be more responsible for their involvement, namely CTI, which measures the type of interaction between teachers and children, and SDA, which measures the quality of supervision that teachers exert over daily activities, including tasks. In our example the type of SDA had by far the strongest effect. In other words, children left on their own with poor teacher supervision may not succeed in finishing a task. When teachers possess good supervision qualities children are more likely to get positively involved among themselves to achieve any particular task.

 Progress box twenty three

- In multiple regression the scores on predictor variables (X_1, X_2, etc.) are used to predict scores on a criterion variable (Y').
- Regression lines are calculated by identifying the coefficients (B) which define the slopes for each predictor variable, and the point of intersection common to all regression lines (A).
- In multiple regression the proportion of variance contributed by all predictor variables is compared with residual error using ANOVA.
- The significance of each predictor variable when compared to its standard error is tested individually using t tests for each comparison.
- Standardized beta coefficients allow the relative weights of predictor variables in predicting unit changes on the Y scores to be compared on an identical scale.

24 General linear model

24.1 Introduction

The aim of this final chapter is to introduce a general model that will bring together the main types of statistical analysis. This overall model is called the *general linear model* (GLM).

The term 'general' simply means that the model applies equally to regression analysis and to the analysis of variables in ANOVA.

Turning to the term 'linear', the basic notion is that this refers to the nature of the lines that are used in the statistical models we have considered so far. The assumption of linearity is that the lines are straight lines. We will remind you that the regression equations described in Chapters 22 and 23 were mathematical expressions that define straight lines.

If you look back to Chapter 17, which introduces two-way ANOVA, you will see that the relationships between variables are also based on the slopes of lines. In the graph in Figure 17.1 the different slopes for good readers and less good readers demonstrate that there is an interaction between the two variables.

In Figure 17.2 the fact that the slopes of the lines are identical indicates that there is no interactive relationship between the two variables.

In both multiple regression and ANOVA the assumption is that relationships between variables are defined by the slopes of lines. This is what is meant by a linear model.

24.2 The role of error in GLM

All statistics in psychology are based on a comparison between predicted variance and error variance, expressed as a ratio between them. Error represents the unpredicted variability in human behaviour, which has not been predicted by the researcher.

The results of a research project are more likely to be significant if predicted variance is high and unpredicted error relatively low.

Because the GLM is a general model that accounts for different types of statistical analysis, it always includes the predicted relationships between variables and also an error term.

There are considerable similarities in the way that the error term in GLM is calculated for multiple regression and ANOVA. In both cases, the error term is calculated as error variance. Error variance is also called residual error. This is because error is what is left over after the variance due to predicted variables has been accounted for.

24.3   Application of GLM to linear regression

The GLM has a lot in common with regression equations for multiple regression lines given in Chapter 23. This accounts for the slopes of straight lines representing scores predicted by selected predictor variables.

In multiple regression the variables are often continuous variables, like a numerical rating scale. But it is possible to incorporate a categorical variable, such as attending a nursery school.

24.4   Application of GLM to ANOVA

In ANOVA the independent variables have to be categories. Examples would be the two categories of being given a reading scheme or not being given a reading scheme.

Another similarity between the two models is that ANOVA is used as a test of the effects of variables in regression. It has been argued that there is no essential difference between the predictor variables in multiple regression and the independent variables in ANOVA. The degrees of freedom depend in both cases on the number of predictor variables and the number of independent variables.

24.5   Conclusions

We end this last chapter by identifying some lessons we hope that you will have learned from this book. One lesson is that all types of research are equally valuable.

In *t* tests and ANOVA the research hypothesis predicts differences between experimental conditions selected by the researcher. Selecting experimental conditions to test a research hypothesis has the advantage that the causal effects of several variables can be investigated simultaneously in ANOVA.

In linear regression certain variables are selected as predictor variables. It may be statistically possible that other variables could be regressed in order to achieve the best-fitting regression line. Exploring a research hypothesis predicting relationships between variables has the advantage that many interesting naturally occurring variables can be investigated simultaneously in multiple regression.

This brings us full circle to the first chapter in the book. Understanding a research hypothesis allows the selection of statistical tests to fall into place.

By now you will be able to find your way easily around the Decision Chart. The main distinction is whether a research hypothesis predicts differences between experimental conditions or relationships between variables.

There are a few other questions about related designs (same participants) or unrelated designs (different participants); the number of conditions and variables; and how data are measured.

This is all you need to know to select an appropriate statistical test. Now that you have completed a variety of tests, we hope that statistics will seem a far easier task than you may have thought when you first started out.

Answers to questions

Question 2.1

(a) The independent variable is learning lists of common and rare words.
(b) The dependent variable is recalling words.
(c) If there are higher recall scores in Experimental condition 1, this supports the research hypothesis that it will be easier to recall lists of common words.

Question 4.1

The research hypothesis predicted that participants would have better recall scores for simple texts. The higher mean score for ideas recalled for the simple text in Condition 1 supports the research hypothesis that more ideas will be recalled from simple texts.

Question 4.2

(a) In Table 4.1 three participants scored 5 in Condition 1 and one participant in Condition 2.
(b) In Condition 1 the lowest score was 3 and the highest score was 10.
(c) In Condition 2 the lowest score was 1 and the highest score was 7.

Question 4.3

$p < 0.001$ represents the smallest probability of random scores because there is only 1 in a 1000 probability that the scores are random.

Question 5.1

A rank of 5 has been allocated to the score of 7. The reason is that this is the next highest score after 6, which has been allocated a rank of 4.

Question 6.1

(a) The difference for participant 3 is 2 and the difference for participant 4 is 3.
(b) The mean for Condition 1 is $24 \div 4 = 6$ and the mean for Condition 2 is 3.

Question 6.2

This is a one-tailed hypothesis because it makes a prediction in one direction that students will recall more words when they are listening to music.

Question 6.3

(a) The mean scores are shown in Table A.1.
(b) The blank columns are completed in Table A.1. Note that it is the *Ranks of d* that are assigned to the signed ranks columns although the signs are based on *d*. Because $(-)3$ is the smaller rank total, $W = 3$. $N = 8 - 1$ (tie) $= 7$.
(c) In Table A, looking along the $N = 7$ row the calculated $W = 3$ is smaller than 4 but larger than 2. So the one-tailed hypothesis that texts with short sentences will be easier to comprehend is supported ($p < 0.05$). This result is borne out by the plus signs in favour of condition 1 (short sentences).

Table A.1   Wilcoxon test (Question 6.3)

	Scores (1)	Scores (2)	d	Ranks of d	Signed ranks (plus)	Signed ranks (minus)
	7	8	−1	1		−1
	10	6	+4	4.5	+4.5	
	13	4	+9	7	+7	
	8	4	+4	4.5	+4.5	
	7	7	0	(tie)	—	
	8	10	−2	2		−2
	6	3	+3	3	+3	
	10	3	+7	6	+6	
Means	8.63	5.63		Ranks totals	(+)25	(−)3

Question 7.1

It is not possible to calculate differences between the two conditions because groups of different participants are doing only one condition each.

Question 7.2

One group of different participants would see the text with a title and another group of different participants would see the text without a title. If the same participants saw both texts, they would find it impossible to forget the title in the no title condition.

Question 7.3

(a) Look at the overall ranks of scores in Table A.2. Check that the lowest rank of 1 is allocated to the lowest score of 1 and that the highest rank of 12 is allocated to the highest score of 20.
(b) The rank totals are shown separately for each condition.
(c) The lower rank total for the left-hand condition indicates that lower (i.e. quicker) times are taken to recognize words on the left-hand side of the screen. This supports the research hypothesis.

Table A.2   Mann–Whitney test (unrelated)

Left-hand condition		Right-hand condition	
Scores	*Ranks*	*Scores*	*Ranks*
9	10	8	9
3	3	5	4.5
2	2	7	8
6	6.5	20	12
1	1	11	11
5	4.5	6	6.5
Rank totals	$T_1 = 27$		$T_2 = 51$

Question 8.1

(a) $5 \times 5 = 25$
(b) $-5 \times -5 = 25$
(c) $-1 \times -1 = 1$
(d) $3 \times 3 = 9$

Question 9.1

For Condition 1 the mean is $28 \div 4 = 7$, for Condition 2 it is 7.5.

Question 9.2

The hypothesis is one-tailed because it predicts in one direction – that more words will be recalled from a simple text.

Question 9.3

All the answers to (a)–(e) are shown in Table A.3.

Table A.3 t test (related) (Question 9.3)

Participants	Condition 1	Condition 2	d	d^2
1	6	2	4	16
2	7	1	6	36
3	8	3	5	25
4	10	4	6	36
5	8	3	5	25
6	8	2	6	36
7	5	7	−2	4
8	3	4	−1	1
Means	6.88	3.25	$\Sigma d = 29$	$\Sigma d^2 = 179$

Question 10.1

The two scores of 5 do not represent tied scores because the two scores come from different groups of participants.

Question 11.1

Table A.4   Ranked scores

	Conditions 1		Condition 2		Condition 3	
Participants	Scores	Ranks	Scores	Ranks	Scores	Ranks
5	3	1	7	3	5	2
6	3	1.5	3	1.5	6	3

Note that for participant 5 the highest score of 7 is in Condition 2 so this is assigned the highest rank of 3. For participant 6 the two scores of 3 are assigned tied ranks of 1.5.

Question 11.2

(a) For Condition 1 the mean is $8 \div 4 = 2$, for Condition 2 it is 5, and for Condition 3 it is 5.5.
(b) These means indicate that fewer rare words were recalled in Condition 1 than common or very common words in the other two conditions.

Question 11.3

(a) For Condition 1 the mean is 3.6, for Condition 2 it is 6.6, for Condition 3 it is 7.
(b) The independent variable is the colour in which the prose passages were printed. The dependent variable is the number of ideas recalled from each passage.
(c) The Friedman test for related designs is appropriate because the *same* five subjects read all *three* prose passages.
(d) The horizontal ranks across the three conditions for each participant are shown in Table A.5.
(e) The rank totals for each condition are shown in Table A.5.

Table A.5   Friedman test (Question 11.3)

Scores (1)	Ranks	Scores (2)	Ranks	Scores (3)	Ranks
4	1	5	2	6	3
2	1	7	2.5	7	2.5
6	1.5	6	1.5	8	3
3	1	7	3	5	2
3	1	8	2	9	3
	$T_1 = 5.5$		$T_2 = 11$		$T_3 = 13.5$

Question 12.1

(a) The higher rank total of 39 for Condition 3 indicates that more very common words were recalled than rare words in Condition 1.
(b) For Condition 1 the mean is 1.5, for Condition 2 it is 5, and for Condition 3 it is 7.5. These means also indicate that more very common words (Condition 3) were recalled than rare words (Condition 1).

Question 13.1

(a) The missing score 4 is 16.
(b) The *df* are $4 - 1 = 3$. This reflects the fact that three out of the four scores in Table 13.3 can vary. Given three scores and the total, the fourth score is predictable and so cannot vary.

Question 13.2

(a) Only two participants had a score of 1. This is quite an extreme score in the normal distribution.
(b) Five participants had a score of 6, which is quite near the centre of the distribution of scores.

Question 15.1

The three presentation rates should be presented in different orders. The aim is to counterbalance the order of conditions when all the conditions are presented to the same participants.

Question 17.1

The totals of 9 and 16 represent the main effect of Variable B: less good readers $(2 + 7 = 9)$ and good readers $(8 + 8 = 16)$.

Question 18.1

Group 1 Illustrated texts (A_1) with title (B_1).
Group 2 Illustrated texts (A_1) with no title (B_2).
Group 3 Non-illustrated texts (A_2) with title (B_1).
Group 4 Non-illustrated texts (A_2) with no title (B_2).

Question 19.1

Condition 1 Illustrated texts (A_1) with title (B_1).
Condition 2 Illustrated texts (A_1) with no title (B_2).
Condition 3 Non-illustrated texts (A_2) with title (B_1).
Condition 4 Non-illustrated texts (A_2) with no title (B_2).

Question 20.1

(a) The two categories for Variable A were being given favourable instructions or danger warnings about helping strangers.
(b) The two categories for Variable B were the number of participants who were observed helping a stranger or not helping stranger.

Question 20.2

(a) In cell 3, there were 23 social science students who reported mixed study patterns.
(b) In cell 5, there were 8 technology students who reported irregular study patterns.
(c) The total for regular study patterns was 16.
(d) The total for mixed study patterns was 47.
(e) The total of technology students was 42.

Question 20.3

(a) The relevant totals for cell 2 are the total of 44 social science students and the total of 23 students who reported irregular study patterns.
(b) The relevant totals for cell 3 are the total of 44 social science students and the total of 47 students who reported mixed study patterns.
(c) The relevant totals for cell 4 are the total of 42 technology students and the total of 16 students who reported regular study patterns.
(d) The relevant total for cell 6 are the total of 42 technology students and the total of 47 students who reported mixed study patterns.

Question 21.1

(a) There is usually a high positive correlation between the people's height and the size of their shoes. This is not a perfect correlation because some tall people have very small feet.
(b) There should be a perfect positive correlation between these variables because the number of tickets sold should exactly correspond to the number of customers (unless, of course, some people manage to slip into the cinema without paying!).
(c) There is most unlikely to be any correlation between the two variables of amount of spinach eaten and the amount of money won on the pools – unfortunately!

Question 21.2

(a) In winter, the *lower* the temperature, the *higher* electrical bills are likely to be. This is a negative correlation because low temperatures go with high electricity bills. The variables of temperature and the amounts charged for electricity are moving in opposite directions.
(b) There is likely to be a positive correlation between the amount of rain falling and the number of umbrella sales.

Question 21.3

(a) The correlations should be listed in the order: 0, +0.5, –0.9.
   (i)   0 is the lowest correlation coefficient because it indicates that there is no correlation at all.
   (ii) +0.5 is next highest because +0.5 is exactly half-way between 0 and +1.
   (iii) –0.9 is the highest correlation coefficient because it is only slightly less than a perfect negative correlation of –1.
(b) There is a positive correlation between number of miles in a journey and the cost of a railway ticket. But this will *not* be a perfect correlation because on some lines tickets can cost more or less for different length journeys (+0.5).
(c) There is probably a zero correlation between number of pedestrian crossings and average earnings.
(d) There is likely to be a highly negative correlation between practising the piano and time available for football (–0.9).

Question 21.4

If a researcher predicted that there would be a correlation, but that the correlation might turn out to be either positive or negative, this would be a two-tailed hypothesis making predictions in two directions.

Question 21.5

(a) Three possible relationships between reading and arithmetic are shown in Figure A.1.
(b) It is pretty obvious that there is no direct relationship between a cock crowing and an alarm clock going off. They are explained by another variable (early rising).

Question 22.1

(a) Reading scores (Variable *B*) is the predictor variable.
(b) Arithmetic scores (Variable *A*) is the predicted criterion variable.
(c) It is a convention to refer to the predictor variable (Variable *B*) as *X* and the predicted criterion variable (Variable *A*) as *Y*.

Question 22.2

The three dots on the left of the scatter plot represent children who all obtained very low reading scores of 1 but rather different arithmetic scores. If you look at Table 22.1 you can see that child 4 has a score of 1 for reading combined with a low score of 6 for arithmetic. Child 3 is the odd one out. A low score of 1 for reading

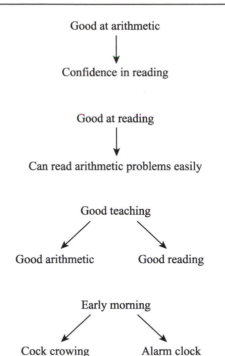

Figure A.1   Relationship between variables (Question 21.5)

would be expected to go with a low arithmetic score. But child 3 has one of the highest arithmetic scores of 12.

Question 23.1

(a) The correlation between Y and X_2 equals 0.52.
(b) The correlation between X_2 and X_2 equals 1. This is because a variable always has a correlation of 1 with itself in the multiple correlation matrix.

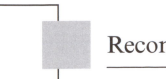

Recommended reading

There are a few books which provide some useful insights into experimental design and statistics.

One general book is *Research Methods and Statistics in Psychology* by Hugh Coolican. This book gives an introduction to designing experiments and other types of research. Ethics is taken into consideration and there are useful hints about describing data and writing up research reports. The statistics are quite simple, but there are other compensations. Another book which covers much of the same ground is *Designing and Reporting Experiments* by Peter Harris.

Siegel's book, *Nonparametric Statistics for the Behavioral Sciences*, is a classic book on non-parametric tests. In fact, it was Siegel who made these tests so popular.

There are also more advanced statistic textbooks. These tend to assume quite a lot of knowledge and tend to be couched in mathematical language. They contain calculations for the Tukey test for looking at comparisons between ANOVA conditions, which is described in Chapter 16. Two recent books are *Doing Quantitative Psychological Research* by David Clark-Carter and *Data Analysis for Psychology* by George Dunbar.

Finally, there are many manuals for computerized statistical packages. One of the most commonly used programs is SPSS, which can be used on either a PC or Macintosh.

References

Brace, N., Kemp, R. and Snelgar, R. (2003) *SPSS for Psychologists*. Basingstoke: Palgrave Macmillan.

Clark-Carter, D. (1997) *Doing Quantitative Psychological Research: From Design to Report*. Hove: Psychology Press.

Coolican, H. (1999) *Research Methods and Statistics in Psychology* (3rd edition). London: Hodder & Stoughton.

Dunbar, G. (1998) *Data Analysis for Psychology*. London: Arnold.

Harris, P. (2002) *Designing and Reporting Experiments in Psychology* (2nd edition). Maidenhead: Open University Press.

Pallant, J. (2001) *SPSS Survival Manual*. Maidenhead: Open University Press.

Siegel, S. (1956) *Nonparametric Statistics for the Behavioral Sciences*. New York: McGraw-Hill.

Statistical tables

Table A Critical values of W at various levels of probability (Wilcoxon)

The statistic W denotes the smaller sum of total signed ranks. For any N (number of participants minus ties) the observed value of W is significant at a given level of significance if it is *equal to* or *less than* the critical values shown in the table.

	Level of significance for one-tailed test					Level of significance for one-tailed test			
	0.05	0.025	0.01	0.005		0.05	0.025	0.01	0.005
	Level of significance for two-tailed test					Level of significance for two-tailed test			
N	0.10	0.05	0.02	0.01	N	0.10	0.05	0.02	0.01
5	1	–	–	–	28	130	117	102	92
6	2	1	–	–	29	141	127	111	100
7	4	2	0	–	30	152	137	120	109
8	6	4	2	0	31	163	148	130	118
9	8	6	3	2	32	175	159	141	128
10	11	8	5	3	33	188	171	151	138
11	14	11	7	5	34	201	183	162	149
12	17	14	10	7	35	214	195	174	160
13	21	17	13	10	36	228	208	186	171
14	26	21	16	13	37	242	222	198	183
15	30	25	20	16	38	256	235	211	195
16	36	30	24	19	39	271	250	224	208
17	41	35	28	23	40	287	264	238	221
18	47	40	33	28	41	303	279	252	234
19	54	46	38	32	42	319	295	267	248
20	60	52	43	37	43	336	311	281	262
21	68	59	49	43	44	353	327	297	277
22	75	66	56	49	45	371	344	313	292
23	83	73	62	55	46	389	361	329	307
24	92	81	69	61	47	408	379	345	323
25	101	90	77	68	48	427	397	362	339
26	110	98	85	76	49	446	415	380	356
27	120	107	93	84	50	466	434	398	373

* Dashes in the body of the table indicate that no decision is possible at the stated level of significance because the numbers of participants are too small.

Table B Critical values of *U* at various levels of probability (Mann–Whitney)

For any n_1 and n_2 the observed value of *U* is significant at a given level of significance if it is *equal to* or *less than* the critical values shown in Tables B(1) and B(2).

Table B(1) Critical values of *U* for a one-tailed test at 0.05; two-tailed test at 0.10*

n_2	1	2	3	4	5	6	7	8	9	10	11	12	13	14	15	16	17	18	19	20
1	–	–	–	–	–	–	–	–	–	–	–	–	–	–	–	–	–	–	0	0
2	–	–	–	–	0	0	0	1	1	1	1	2	2	2	3	3	3	4	4	4
3	–	–	0	0	1	2	2	3	3	4	5	5	6	7	7	8	9	9	10	11
4	–	–	0	1	2	3	4	5	6	7	8	9	10	11	12	14	15	16	17	18
5	–	0	1	2	4	5	6	8	9	11	12	13	15	16	18	19	20	22	23	25
6	–	0	2	3	5	7	8	10	12	14	16	17	19	21	23	25	26	28	30	32
7	–	0	2	4	6	8	11	13	15	17	19	21	24	26	28	30	33	35	37	39
8	–	1	3	5	8	10	13	15	18	20	23	26	28	31	33	36	39	41	44	47
9	–	1	3	6	9	12	15	18	21	24	27	30	33	36	39	42	45	48	51	54
10	–	1	4	7	11	14	17	20	24	27	31	34	37	41	44	48	51	55	58	62
11	–	1	5	8	12	16	19	23	27	31	34	38	42	46	50	54	57	61	65	69
12	–	2	5	9	13	17	21	26	30	34	38	42	47	51	55	60	64	68	72	77
13	–	2	6	10	15	19	24	28	33	37	42	47	51	56	61	65	70	75	80	84
14	–	2	7	11	16	21	26	31	36	41	46	51	56	61	66	71	77	82	87	92
15	–	3	7	12	18	23	28	33	39	44	50	55	61	66	72	77	83	88	94	100
16	–	3	8	14	19	25	30	36	42	48	54	60	65	71	77	83	89	95	101	107
17	–	3	9	15	20	26	33	39	45	51	57	64	70	77	83	89	96	102	109	115
18	–	4	9	16	22	28	35	41	48	55	61	68	75	82	88	95	102	109	116	123
19	0	4	10	17	23	30	37	44	51	58	65	72	80	87	94	101	109	116	123	130
20	0	4	11	18	25	32	39	47	54	62	69	77	84	92	100	107	115	123	130	138

* Dashes in the body of the table indicate that no decision is possible at the stated level of significance because the numbers of participants are too small.

Table B(2) Critical values of U for a one-tailed test at 0.01; two-tailed test at 0.02*.

n_2	n_1																			
	1	2	3	4	5	6	7	8	9	10	11	12	13	14	15	16	17	18	19	20
1	–	–	–	–	–	–	–	–	–	–	–	–	–	–	–	–	–	–	–	–
2	–	–	–	–	–	–	–	–	–	–	–	–	–	0	0	0	0	0	0	1	1
3	–	–	–	–	–	–	0	0	1	1	1	2	2	2	3	3	4	4	4	5
4	–	–	–	–	0	1	1	2	3	3	4	5	5	6	7	7	8	9	9	10
5	–	–	–	0	1	2	3	4	5	6	7	8	9	10	11	12	13	14	15	16
6	–	–	–	1	2	3	4	6	7	8	9	11	12	13	15	16	18	19	20	22
7	–	–	0	1	3	4	6	7	9	11	12	14	16	17	19	21	23	24	26	28
8	–	–	0	2	4	6	7	9	11	13	15	17	20	22	24	26	28	30	32	34
9	–	–	1	3	5	7	9	11	14	16	18	21	23	26	28	31	33	36	38	40
10	–	–	1	3	6	8	11	13	16	19	22	24	27	30	33	36	38	41	44	47
11	–	–	1	4	7	9	12	15	18	22	25	28	31	34	37	41	44	47	50	53
12	–	–	2	5	8	11	14	17	21	24	28	31	35	38	42	46	49	53	56	60
13	–	0	2	5	9	12	16	20	23	27	31	35	39	43	47	51	55	59	63	67
14	–	0	2	6	10	13	17	22	26	30	34	38	43	47	51	56	60	65	69	73
15	–	0	3	7	11	15	19	24	28	33	37	42	47	51	56	61	66	70	75	80
16	–	0	3	7	12	16	21	26	31	36	41	46	51	56	61	66	71	76	82	87
17	–	0	4	8	13	18	23	28	33	38	44	49	55	60	66	71	77	82	88	93
18	–	0	4	9	14	19	24	30	36	41	47	53	59	65	70	76	82	88	94	100
19	–	1	4	9	15	20	26	32	38	44	50	56	63	69	75	82	88	94	101	107
20	–	1	5	10	16	22	28	34	40	47	53	60	67	73	80	87	93	100	107	114

* Dashes in the body of the table indicate that no decision is possible at the stated level of significance because the numbers of participants are too small.

Table C Critical values of *t* at various levels of probability (*t* test)

For any particular *df* the observed value of *t* is significant at a given level of significance if it is *equal to* or *larger than* the critical values shown in the table.

	Level of significance for one-tailed test					
	0.10	*0.05*	*0.025*	*0.01*	*0.005*	*0.0005*
	Level of significance for two-tailed test					
df	*0.20*	*0.10*	*0.05*	*0.02*	*0.01*	*0.001*
1	3.078	6.314	12.706	31.821	63.657	636.619
2	1.886	2.920	4.303	6.965	9.925	31.598
3	1.638	2.353	3.182	4.541	5.841	12.941
4	1.533	2.132	2.776	3.747	4.604	8.610
5	1.476	2.015	2.571	3.365	4.032	6.859
6	1.440	1.943	2.447	3.143	3.707	5.959
7	1.415	1.895	2.365	2.998	3.499	5.405
8	1.397	1.860	2.306	2.896	3.355	5.041
9	1.383	1.833	2.262	2.821	3.250	4.781
10	1.372	1.812	2.228	2.764	3.169	4.587
11	1.363	1.796	2.201	2.718	3.106	4.437
12	1.356	1.782	2.179	2.681	3.055	4.318
13	1.350	1.771	2.160	2.650	3.012	4.221
14	1.345	1.761	2.145	2.624	2.977	4.140
15	1.341	1.753	2.131	2.602	2.947	4.073
16	1.337	1.746	2.120	2.583	2.921	4.015
17	1.333	1.740	2.110	2.567	2.898	3.965
18	1.330	1.734	2.101	2.552	2.878	3.922
19	1.328	1.729	2.093	2.539	2.861	3.883
20	1.325	1.725	2.086	2.528	2.845	3.850
21	1.323	1.721	2.080	2.518	2.831	3.819
22	1.321	1.717	2.074	2.508	2.819	3.792
23	1.319	1.714	2.069	2.500	2.807	3.767
24	1.318	1.711	2.064	2.492	2.797	3.745
25	1.316	1.708	2.060	2.485	2.787	3.725
26	1.315	1.706	2.056	2.479	2.779	3.707
27	1.314	1.703	2.052	2.473	2.771	3.690
28	1.313	1.701	2.048	2.467	2.763	3.674
29	1.311	1.699	2.045	2.462	2.756	3.659
30	1.310	1.697	2.042	2.457	2.750	3.646
40	1.303	1.684	2.021	2.423	2.704	3.551
60	1.296	1.671	2.000	2.390	2.660	3.460
120	1.289	1.658	1.980	2.358	2.617	3.373
∞	1.282	1.645	1.960	2.326	2.576	3.291

N.B. When required *df* is not shown, use the next lowest number, except for very large *df*s (well over 120), when you can use the row for infinity (∞).

Table D Critical values of χ_r^2 for three conditions at various levels of probability (Friedman)

For any N the observed value of χ_r^2 is significant at a given level of significance if it is *equal to* or *larger than* the critical values shown in Table D.

$N = 2$		$N = 3$		$N = 4$		$N = 5$	
χ_r^2	p	χ_r^2	p	χ_r^2	p	χ_r^2	p
4	0.167	2.667	0.361	2.0	0.431	1.6	0.522
		4.667	0.194	3.5	0.273	2.8	0.367
		6.000	0.028	4.5	0.125	3.6	0.182
				6.0	0.069	4.8	0.124
				6.5	0.042	5.2	0.093
				8.0	0.0046	6.4	0.039
						7.6	0.024
						8.4	0.0085
						10.0	0.00077

$N = 6$		$N = 7$		$N = 8$		$N = 9$	
χ_r^2	p	χ_r^2	p	χ_r^2	p	χ_r^2	p
4.00	0.184	3.429	0.237	3.00	0.285	2.667	0.328
4.33	0.142	3.714	0.192	3.25	0.236	2.889	0.278
5.33	0.072	4.571	0.112	4.00	0.149	3.556	0.187
6.33	0.052	5.429	0.085	4.75	0.120	4.222	0.154
7.00	0.029	6.000	0.052	5.25	0.079	4.667	0.107
8.33	0.012	7.143	0.027	6.25	0.047	5.556	0.069
9.00	0.0081	7.714	0.021	6.75	0.038	6.000	0.057
9.33	0.0055	8.000	0.016	7.00	0.030	6.222	0.048
10.33	0.0017	8.857	0.0084	7.75	0.018	6.889	0.031
12.00	0.00013	10.286	0.0036	9.00	0.0099	8.000	0.019
		10.571	0.0027	9.25	0.0080	8.222	0.016
		11.143	0.0012	9.75	0.0048	8.667	0.010
		12.286	0.00032	10.75	0.0024	9.556	0.0060
		14.000	0.000021	12.00	0.0011	10.667	0.0035
				12.25	0.00086	10.889	0.0029
				13.00	0.00026	11.556	0.0013
				14.25	0.000061	12.667	0.00066
				16.00	0.0000036	13.556	0.00035
						14.000	0.00020
						14.222	0.000097
						14.889	0.000054
						16.222	0.000011
						18.000	0.0000006

Table E   Critical values of χ^2 at various levels of probability (chi-square)

For any particular *df* the observed value of χ^2 is significant at a given level of significance if it is *equal to* or *larger than* the critical values shown in the table.

df	0.10	0.05	0.02	0.01	0.001
1	2.71	3.84	5.41	6.64	10.83
2	4.60	5.99	7.82	9.21	13.82
3	6.25	7.82	9.84	11.34	16.27
4	7.78	9.49	11.67	13.28	18.46
5	9.24	11.07	13.39	15.09	20.52
6	10.64	12.59	15.03	16.81	22.46
7	12.02	14.07	16.62	18.48	24.32
8	13.36	15.51	18.17	20.09	26.12
9	14.68	16.92	19.68	21.67	27.88
10	15.99	18.31	21.16	23.21	29.59
11	17.28	19.68	22.62	24.72	31.26
12	18.55	21.03	24.05	26.22	32.91
13	19.81	22.36	25.47	27.69	34.53
14	21.06	23.68	26.87	29.14	36.12
15	22.31	25.00	28.26	30.58	37.70
16	23.54	26.30	29.63	32.00	39.29
17	24.77	27.59	31.00	33.41	40.75
18	25.99	28.87	32.35	34.80	42.31
19	27.20	30.14	33.69	36.19	43.82
20	28.41	31.41	35.02	37.57	45.32
21	29.62	32.67	36.34	38.93	46.80
22	30.81	33.92	37.66	40.29	48.27
23	32.01	35.17	38.97	41.64	49.73
24	33.20	36.42	40.27	42.98	51.18
25	34.38	37.65	41.57	44.31	52.62
26	35.56	38.88	42.86	45.64	54.05
27	36.74	40.11	44.14	46.97	55.48
28	37.92	41.34	45.42	48.28	56.89
29	39.09	42.56	46.69	49.59	58.30
30	40.26	43.77	47.96	50.89	59.70

Table F Critical values of *H* at various levels of probability (Kruskal–Wallis)

For any n_1, n_2, n_3 the observed value of *H* is significant at a given level of significance if it is *equal to* or *larger than* the critical values shown in the table.

n_1	n_2	n_3	*H*	*p*	n_1	n_2	n_3	*H*	*p*
2	1	1	2.7000	0.500	4	3	1	5.8333	0.021
2	2	1	3.6000	0.200				5.2083	0.050
								5.0000	0.057
2	2	2	4.5714	0.067				4.0556	0.093
			3.7143	0.200				3.8889	0.129
3	1	1	3.2000	0.300	4	3	2	6.4444	0.008
3	2	1	4.2857	0.100				6.3000	0.011
			3.8571	0.133				5.4444	0.046
3	2	2	5.3572	0.029				5.4000	0.051
			4.7143	0.048				4.5111	0.098
			4.5000	0.067				4.4444	0.102
			4.4643	0.105	4	3	3	6.7455	0.010
3	3	1	5.1429	0.043				6.7091	0.013
			4.5714	0.100				5.7909	0.046
			4.0000	0.129				5.7273	0.050
3	3	2	6.2500	0.011				4.7091	0.092
			5.3611	0.032				4.7000	0.101
			5.1389	0.061	4	4	1	6.6667	0.010
			4.5556	0.100				6.1667	0.022
			4.2500	0.121				4.9667	0.048
3	3	3	7.2000	0.004				4.8667	0.054
			6.4889	0.011				4.1667	0.082
			5.6889	0.029				4.0667	0.102
			5.6000	0.050	4	4	2	7.0364	0.006
			5.0667	0.086				6.8727	0.011
			4.6222	0.100				5.4545	0.046
4	1	1	3.5714	0.200				5.2364	0.052
4	2	1	4.8214	0.057				4.5545	0.098
			4.5000	0.076				4.4455	0.103
			4.0179	0.114	4	4	3	7.1439	0.010
4	2	2	6.0000	0.014				7.1364	0.011
			5.3333	0.033				5.5985	0.049
			5.1250	0.052				5.5758	0.051
			4.4583	0.100				4.5455	0.099
								4.4773	0.102

Table F   *(continued)*

Size of groups					Size of groups				
n_1	n_2	n_3	H	p	n_1	n_2	n_3	H	p
4	4	4	7.6538	0.008	5	4	2	7.2045	0.009
			7.5385	0.011				7.1182	0.010
			5.6923	0.049				5.2727	0.049
			5.6538	0.054				5.2682	0.050
			4.6539	0.097				4.5409	0.098
			4.5001	0.104				4.5182	0.101
5	1	1	3.8571	0.143	5	4	3	7.4449	0.010
5	2	1	5.2500	0.036				7.3949	0.011
			5.0000	0.048				5.6564	0.049
			4.4500	0.071				5.6308	0.050
			4.2000	0.095				4.5487	0.099
			4.0500	0.119	5	4	4	7.7604	0.009
5	2	2	6.5333	0.008				7.7440	0.011
			6.1333	0.013				5.6571	0.049
			5.1600	0.034				5.6176	0.050
			5.0400	0.056				4.6187	0.100
			4.3733	0.090	5	5	1	7.3091	0.009
			4.2933	0.122				6.8364	0.011
5	3	1	6.4000	0.012				5.1273	0.046
			4.9600	0.048				4.9091	0.053
			4.8711	0.052				4.1091	0.086
			4.0178	0.095	5	5	2	7.3385	0.010
			3.8400	0.123				7.2692	0.010
5	3	2	6.9091	0.009				5.3385	0.047
			6.8218	0.010				5.2462	0.051
			5.2509	0.049				4.6231	0.097
			5.1055	0.052	5	5	3	7.5780	0.010
			4.6509	0.091				7.5429	0.010
			4.4945	0.101				5.7055	0.046
5	3	3	7.0788	0.009				5.6264	0.051
			6.9818	0.011				4.5451	0.100
			5.6485	0.049	5	5	4	7.8229	0.010
			5.5152	0.051				7.7914	0.010
			4.5333	0.097				5.6657	0.049
			4.4121	0.109				5.6429	0.050
5	4	1	6.9545	0.008				4.5229	0.099
			6.8400	0.011	5	5	5	8.0000	0.009
			4.9855	0.044				7.9800	0.010
			4.8600	0.056				5.7800	0.049
			3.9873	0.098				5.6600	0.051
			3.9600	0.102				4.5600	0.100

Table G   Critical values of *F* at various levels of probability (ANOVA)

For any v_1 and v_2 the observed value of *F* is significant at a given level of significance if it is *equal to* or *larger than* the critical values shown in Tables G(1)–G(2).

Table G(1)   Critical values of *F* at $p < 0.05$

v_2	1	2	3	4	5	6	7	8	10	12	24	∞
5	6.61	5.79	5.41	5.19	5.05	4.95	4.88	4.82	4.74	4.68	4.53	4.36
6	5.99	5.14	4.76	4.53	4.39	4.28	4.21	4.15	4.06	4.00	3.84	3.67
7	5.59	4.74	4.35	4.12	3.97	3.87	3.79	3.73	3.64	3.57	3.41	3.23
8	5.32	4.46	4.07	3.84	3.69	3.58	3.50	3.44	3.35	3.28	3.12	2.93
9	5.12	4.26	3.86	3.63	3.48	3.37	3.29	3.23	3.14	3.07	2.90	2.71
10	4.96	4.10	3.71	3.48	3.33	3.22	3.14	3.07	2.98	2.91	2.74	2.54
11	4.84	3.98	3.59	3.36	3.20	3.09	3.01	2.95	2.85	2.79	2.61	2.40
12	4.75	3.89	3.49	3.26	3.11	3.00	2.91	2.85	2.75	2.69	2.51	2.30
13	4.67	3.81	3.41	3.18	3.03	2.92	2.83	2.77	2.67	2.60	2.42	2.21
14	4.60	3.74	3.34	3.11	2.96	2.85	2.76	2.70	2.60	2.53	2.35	2.13
15	4.54	3.68	3.29	3.06	2.90	2.79	2.71	2.64	2.54	2.48	2.29	2.07
16	4.49	3.63	3.24	3.01	2.85	2.74	2.66	2.59	2.49	2.42	2.24	2.01
17	4.45	3.59	3.20	2.96	2.81	2.70	2.61	2.55	2.45	2.38	2.19	1.96
18	4.41	3.55	3.16	2.93	2.77	2.66	2.58	2.51	2.41	2.34	2.15	1.92
19	4.38	3.52	3.13	2.90	2.74	2.63	2.54	2.48	2.38	2.31	2.11	1.88
20	4.35	3.49	3.10	2.87	2.71	2.60	2.51	2.45	2.35	2.28	2.08	1.84
21	4.32	3.47	3.07	2.84	2.68	2.57	2.49	2.42	2.32	2.25	2.05	1.81
22	4.30	3.44	3.05	2.82	2.66	2.55	2.46	2.40	2.30	2.23	2.03	1.78
23	4.28	3.42	3.03	2.80	2.64	2.53	2.44	2.37	2.27	2.20	2.00	1.76
24	4.26	3.40	3.01	2.78	2.62	2.51	2.42	2.36	2.25	2.18	1.98	1.73
25	4.24	3.39	2.99	2.76	2.60	2.49	2.40	2.34	2.24	2.16	1.96	1.71
26	4.23	3.37	2.98	2.74	2.59	2.47	2.39	2.32	2.22	2.15	1.95	1.69
27	4.21	3.35	2.96	2.73	2.57	2.46	2.37	2.31	2.20	2.13	1.93	1.67
28	4.20	3.34	2.95	2.71	2.56	2.45	2.36	2.29	2.19	2.12	1.91	1.65
29	4.18	3.33	2.93	2.70	2.55	2.43	2.35	2.28	2.18	2.10	1.90	1.64
30	4.17	3.32	2.92	2.69	2.53	2.42	2.33	2.27	2.16	2.09	1.89	1.62
32	4.15	3.29	2.90	2.67	2.51	2.40	2.31	2.24	2.14	2.07	1.86	1.59
34	4.13	3.28	2.88	2.65	2.49	2.38	2.29	2.23	2.12	2.05	1.84	1.57
36	4.11	3.26	2.87	2.63	2.48	2.36	2.28	2.21	2.11	2.03	1.82	1.55
38	4.10	3.24	2.85	2.62	2.46	2.35	2.26	2.19	2.09	2.02	1.81	1.53
40	4.08	3.23	2.84	2.61	2.45	2.34	2.25	2.18	2.08	2.00	1.79	1.51
60	4.00	3.15	2.76	2.53	2.37	2.25	2.17	2.10	1.99	1.92	1.70	1.39
120	3.92	3.07	2.68	2.45	2.29	2.18	2.09	2.02	1.91	1.83	1.61	1.25
∞	3.84	3.00	2.60	2.37	2.21	2.10	2.01	1.94	1.83	1.75	1.52	1.00

N.B. When the required *df*s are not shown use the next lowest number. For very large *df*s (well over 120) you can use infinity (∞).

Table G(2)   Critical values of F at $p < 0.01$

v_2	v_1											
	1	2	3	4	5	6	7	8	10	12	24	∞
5	16.26	13.27	12.06	11.39	10.97	10.67	10.46	10.29	10.05	9.89	9.47	9.02
6	13.74	10.92	9.78	9.15	8.75	8.47	8.26	8.10	7.87	7.72	7.31	6.88
7	12.25	9.55	8.45	7.85	7.46	7.19	6.99	6.84	6.62	6.47	6.07	5.65
8	11.26	8.65	7.59	7.01	6.63	6.37	6.18	6.03	5.81	5.67	5.28	4.86
9	10.56	8.02	6.99	6.42	6.06	5.80	5.61	5.47	5.26	5.11	4.73	4.31
10	10.04	7.56	6.55	5.99	5.64	5.39	5.20	5.06	4.85	4.71	4.33	3.91
11	9.65	7.21	6.22	5.67	5.32	5.07	4.89	4.74	4.54	4.40	4.02	3.60
12	9.33	6.93	5.95	5.41	5.06	4.82	4.64	4.50	4.30	4.16	3.78	3.36
13	9.07	6.70	5.74	5.21	4.86	4.62	4.44	4.30	4.10	3.96	3.59	3.17
14	8.86	6.51	5.56	5.04	4.70	4.46	4.28	4.14	3.94	3.80	3.43	3.00
15	8.68	6.36	5.42	4.89	4.56	4.32	4.14	4.00	3.80	3.67	3.29	2.87
16	8.53	6.23	5.29	4.77	4.44	4.20	4.03	3.89	3.69	3.55	3.18	2.75
17	8.40	6.11	5.18	4.67	4.34	4.10	3.93	3.79	3.59	3.46	3.08	2.65
18	8.29	6.01	5.09	4.58	4.25	4.01	3.84	3.71	3.51	3.37	3.00	2.57
19	8.18	5.93	5.01	4.50	4.17	3.94	3.77	3.63	3.43	3.30	2.92	2.49
20	8.10	5.85	4.94	4.43	4.10	3.87	3.70	3.56	3.37	3.23	2.86	2.42
21	8.02	5.78	4.87	4.37	4.04	3.81	3.64	3.51	3.31	3.17	2.80	2.36
22	7.95	5.72	4.82	4.31	3.99	3.76	3.59	3.45	3.26	3.12	2.75	2.31
23	7.88	5.66	4.76	4.26	3.94	3.71	3.54	3.41	3.21	3.07	2.70	2.26
24	7.82	5.61	4.72	4.22	3.90	3.67	3.50	3.36	3.17	3.03	2.66	2.21
25	7.77	5.57	4.68	4.18	3.86	3.63	3.46	3.32	3.13	2.99	2.62	2.17
26	7.72	5.53	4.64	4.14	3.82	3.59	3.42	3.29	3.09	2.96	2.58	2.13
27	7.68	5.49	4.60	4.11	3.78	3.56	3.39	3.26	3.06	2.93	2.55	2.10
28	7.64	5.45	4.57	4.07	3.75	3.53	3.36	3.23	3.03	2.90	2.52	2.06
29	7.60	5.42	4.54	4.04	3.73	3.50	3.33	3.20	3.00	2.87	2.49	2.03
30	7.56	5.39	4.51	4.02	3.70	3.47	3.30	3.17	2.98	2.84	2.47	2.01
32	7.50	5.34	4.46	3.97	3.65	3.43	3.26	3.13	2.93	2.80	2.42	1.96
34	7.45	5.29	4.42	3.93	3.61	3.39	3.22	3.09	2.90	2.76	2.38	1.91
36	7.40	5.25	4.38	3.89	3.58	3.35	3.18	3.05	2.86	2.72	2.35	1.87
38	7.35	5.21	4.34	3.86	3.54	3.32	3.15	3.02	2.83	2.69	2.32	1.84
40	7.31	5.18	4.31	3.83	3.51	3.29	3.12	2.99	2.80	2.66	2.29	1.80
60	7.08	4.98	4.13	3.65	3.34	3.12	2.95	2.82	2.63	2.50	2.12	1.60
120	6.85	4.79	3.95	3.48	3.17	2.96	2.79	2.66	2.47	2.34	1.95	1.38
∞	6.63	4.61	3.78	3.32	3.02	2.80	2.64	2.51	2.32	2.18	1.79	1.00

Table H   Critical values of *r* at various levels of probability (Pearson correlation)

The observed value of *r* is significant at a given level of significance if it is *equal* to or *larger* than the critical values shown in the table

	Level of significance for one-tailed test				
	.05	.025	.01	.005	.0005
	Level of significance for two-tailed test				
df	.10	.05	.02	.01	.001
1	.9877	.9969	.9995	.9999	1.0000
2	.9000	.9500	.9800	.9900	.9990
3	.8054	.8783	.9343	.9587	.9912
4	.7293	.8114	.8822	.9172	.9741
5	.6694	.7545	.8329	.8745	.9507
6	.6215	.7067	.7887	.8343	.9249
7	.5822	.6664	.7498	.7977	.8982
8	.5494	.6319	.7155	.7646	.8721
9	.5214	.6021	.6851	.7348	.8471
10	.4973	.5760	.6581	.7079	.8233
11	.4762	.5529	.6339	.6835	.8010
12	.4575	.5324	.6120	.6614	.7800
13	.4409	.5139	.5923	.6411	.7603
14	.4259	.4973	.5742	.6226	.7420
15	.4124	.4821	.5577	.6055	.7246
16	.4000	.4683	.5425	.5897	.7084
17	.3887	.4555	.5285	.5751	.6932
18	.3783	.4438	.5155	.5614	.6787
19	.3687	.4329	.5034	.5487	.6652
20	.3598	.4227	.4921	.5368	.6524
25	.3233	.3809	.4451	.4869	.5974
30	.2960	.3494	.4093	.4487	.5541
35	.2746	.3246	.3810	.4182	.5189
40	.2573	.3044	.3578	.3932	.4896
45	.2428	.2875	.3384	.3721	.4648
50	.2306	.2732	.3218	.3541	.4433
60	.2108	.2500	.2948	.3248	.4078
70	.1954	.2319	.2737	.3017	.3799
80	.1829	.2172	.2565	.2830	.3568
90	.1726	.2050	.2422	.2673	.3375
100	.1638	.1946	.2301	.2540	.3211

N.B. When there is no exact *df* use the next lowest number.

Index

Related books from Open University Press

Purchase from www.openup.co.uk or order through your local bookseller

SPSS SURVIVAL MANUAL
A STEP BY STEP GUIDE TO DATA ANALYSIS
USING SPSS FOR WINDOWS (VERSION 12)

Julie Pallant

The *SPSS Survival Manual* throws a lifeline to students and researchers grappling with the SPSS data analysis software.

In this fully revised edition of her bestselling text, Julie Pallant guides you through the entire research process, helping you choose the right data analysis technique for your project. From the formulation of research questions, to the design of the study and analysis of data, to reporting the results, Julie discusses basic and advanced statistical techniques. She outlines each technique clearly, with step-by-step procedures for performing the analysis, a detailed guide to interpreting SPSS output and an example of how to present the results in a report.

Statistical techniques covered include: descriptive statistics; correlation; multiple regression; logistic regression; factor analysis; T-tests; analysis of variance; multivariate analysis of variance; analysis of covariance; non-parametric tests.

For both beginners and experienced SPSS users in psychology, education, business, sociology, health and related disciplines, the *SPSS Survival Manual* is an essential guide. Illustrated with screen grabs, examples of output and tips, it is supported by a website with sample data and guidelines on report writing. This second edition includes new examples, a new section on logistic regression and fully integrated coverage of SPSS version 12.

Contents

336pp   0 335 21640 4 (Spiral Bound)

ADVANCED QUANTITATIVE DATA ANALYSIS

Duncan Cramer

- What do advanced statistical techniques do?
- When is it appropriate to use them?
- How are they carried out and reported?

There are a variety of statistical techniques used to analyse quantitative data that masters students, advanced undergraduates and researchers in the social sciences are expected to be able to understand and undertake. This book explains these techniques, when it is appropriate to use them, how to carry them out and how to write up the results. Most books which describe these techniques do so at too advanced or technical a level to be readily understood by many students who need to use them. In contrast the following features characterise this book:

- Concise and accessible introduction to calculating and interpreting advanced statistical techniques
- Use of a small data set of simple numbers specifically designed to illustrate the nature and manual calculation of the most important statistics in each technique
- Succinct illustration of writing up the results of these analyses
- Minimum of mathematical, statistical and technical notation
- Annotated bibliography and glossary of key concepts

Commonly used software is introduced, and instructions are presented for carrying out analyses and interpreting the output using the computer programs of SPSS Release 11 for Windows and a version of LISREL 8.51, which is freely available online.

Designed as a textbook for postgraduate and advanced undergraduate courses across the socio-behavioural sciences, this book will also serve as a personal reference for researchers in disciplines such as sociology and psychology.

Contents

Series editor's foreword – Preface – Introduction – PART 1: Grouping quantitative variables together – Exploratory factor analysis – Confirmatory factor analysis – Cluster analysis – PART 2: Explaining the variance of a quantitative variable – Stepwise multiple regression – Hierarchical multiple regression – PART 3: Sequencing the relationships between three or more quantitative variables – Path analysis assuming no measurement error – Path analysis accounting for measurement error – PART 4: Explaining the probability of a dichotomous variable – Binary logistic regression – PART 5: Testing differences between group means – An introduction to analysis of variance and covariance – Unrelated one-way analysis of covariance – Unrelated two-way analysis of variance – PART 6: Discriminating between groups – Discriminant analysis – PART 7: Analysing frequency tables with three or more qualitative variables – Log-linear analysis – Glossary – References – Index.

288pp   0 335 20059 1 (Paperback)   0 335 20062 1 (Hardback)

HANDBOOK OF HEALTH RESEARCH METHODS
INVESTIGATION, MEASUREMENT
AND ANALYSIS

Ann Bowling and Shah Ebrahim

- Which research method should I use to evaluate services?
- How do I design a questionnaire?
- How do I conduct a systematic review of research?

This handbook helps researchers to plan, carry out, and analyse health research, and evaluate the quality of research studies. The book takes a multidisciplinary approach to enable researchers from different disciplines to work side by side in the investigation of population health, the evaluation of health care, and in health care delivery.

Handbook of Health Research Methods is an essential tool for researchers and post-graduate students taking masters courses, or undertaking doctoral programmes, in health services evaluation, health sciences, health management, public health, nursing, sociology, biology, medicine and epidemiology. However, the book also appeals to health professionals who wish to broaden their knowledge of research methods in order to make effective policy and practice decisions.

Contributors
Joy Adamson, Geraldine Barrett, Jane P. Biddulph, Ann Bowling, Sara Brookes, Jackie Brown, Simon Carter, Michel P. Coleman, Paul Cullinan, George Davey Smith, Paul Dieppe, Jenny Donovan, Craig Duncan, Shah Ebrahim, Vikki Entwistle, Clare Harries, Lesley Henderson, Kelvyn Jones, Olga Kostopoulou, Sarah J. Lewis, Richard Martin, Martin McKee, Graham Moon, Ellen Nolte, Alan O'Rourke, Ann Oakley, Tim Peters, Tina Ramkalawan, Caroline Sanders, Mary Shaw, Andrew Steptoe, Jonathan Sterne, Anne Stiggelbout, S.V. Subramanian, Kate Tilling, Liz Twigg, Suzanne Wait.

Ann Bowling is Professor of Health Services Research in the Department of Primary Care and Population Sciences at University College London, and has a part second-ment to the MRC Health Services Research Collaboration, University of Bristol. Her other publications with Open University Press include: *Measuring Disease* (2001), *Research Methods in Health* (2002) and *Measuring Health* (2004).

Contents
Section 1: Introduction – Introduction: Research on health and health care – Describing and evaluating health systems – *Section 2: Multidisciplinary methods of investigation* – Evidence based health care: Systematic reviews – Critical appraisal – Features and designs of randomised and non-randomised controlled trials and non-randomised experimental designs – Epidemiological study designs in health care research and evaluation – Finding and using secondary data on the health and health care of populations – Quantitative social science: The survey – Approaches to qualitative data collection in social science – Combined qualitative and quantitative designs – Design and analysis of social intervention studies in health research – Area-based studies and the evaluation of multilevel influences on health outcomes – Mathematical models in health care – Economic evaluation of health care – *Section 3: Multidisciplinary research measurement* – Psychological approaches to measuring and modelling clinical decision making – Approaches to measuring patients' decision making – Techniques of questionnaire design – Measuring health outcomes from the patient's perspective – Genetics, health and population genetics research – Tools of psychosocial biology and health care research – *Section 4: Data analysis* – Key issues in the statistical analysis of quantitative data in research on health and health services – Key issues in the analysis of qualitative data on health services research – *Section 5: Essential issues to consider when conducting research* – Involving service users in health services research – Ethical and political issues in the conduct of research – Training for research – General glossary – General further reading – Index.

640pp   0 335 21460 6 (Paperback)   0 335 21461 4 (Hardback)

REFLECTIONS ON RESEARCH
THE REALITIES OF DOING RESEARCH IN THE SOCIAL SCIENCES

Nina Hallowell, Julia Lawton and Susan Gregory

- What is it really like to do social science research?
- In what ways can research go wrong and what can you do to put it right again?
- How do research methods and research ethics relate in practice?

This is a 'how it went' rather than a 'how to do' research methods book. It is based upon the reflections and experiences of a wide range of established social researchers, the majority of whom undertake research in the field of health care. By drawing upon anecdotal accounts of setting up research projects, negotiating access, gathering data and disseminating findings, the book highlights the practical and ethical complexities involved in the conduct of empirically based research.

By focussing upon the real-life experiences of social science researchers *Reflections on Research* provides insight into the day-to-day realities of conducting research – the pleasures and the pitfalls. As such, it is essential reading for all students and researchers in the social sciences as well as academics and professionals interested in research and research ethics.

Contributors
Priscilla Alderson, Kathryn Backett-Milburn, Rosaline Barbour, Hannah Bradby, Elizabeth Chapman, Susan Cox, Sarah Cunningham-Burley, Gill Dunne, Susan Eley, Elizabeth Ettorre, Catherine Exley, Calliope (Bobbie) Farsides, Claire Foster, Jonathan Gabe, Wendy Gnich, Trudy Goodenough, Susan Gregory, Rachel Grellier, Nina Hallowell, Khim Horton, Julie Kent, Julia Lawton, Abby Lippman, Liz Lobb, Lesley Lockyer, Alice Lovell, Marion McAllister, Richard Mitchell, Virginia Morrow, Melissa Nash, Odette Parry, Stephen Platt, Laura Potts, Shirley Prendergast, Martin Richards, Deborah Ritchie, Ann Robertson, Susan Robinson, Tom Shakespeare, Hilary Thomas, Stefan Timmermans, Kay Tisdall, Jonathan Tritter, Julia Twigg, Clare Williams, Emma Williamson.

Contents
Research in practice or doing the business – Emotions – Self – Others – Control – Reflections on research: ethics in practice – References – Index.

176pp   0 335 21309 X (Paperback)   0 335 213103 (Hardback)

APPROACHES TO PSYCHOLOGY
FOURTH EDITION

William Glassman and Marilyn Hadad

Review of the Third Edition

> Nowhere else is there such thorough coverage of the major perspectives in their historical context. Glassman's clear, consistent and utterly coherent style provides interest through anecdotes, fables, everyday experiences and concrete psychological research examples.
>
> *The Times Higher Education Supplement*

This revised and expanded edition of *Approaches to Psychology* builds on the wide appeal of the earlier editions. It explains what the discipline of psychology is, how it developed and how it can contribute to the understanding of human behaviour and experience.

This book introduces students to the five major conceptual frameworks or "approaches" to psychology: **biological**, **behaviourist**, **cognitive**, **psychodynamic** and **humanistic**. The methods, theories and assumptions of each approach is explored so that the reader builds an understanding of psychology as it applies to human development, social and abnormal behaviour.

New to this edition:

* Brand new layout with more illustrations and two colour design
* Case studies that run throughout the book
* Increased coverage of social psychology
* Enhanced treatment of cross-cultural issues
* New work on evolutionary psychology
* Online Learning Centre (OLC) with student support material, instructor test bank (www.openup.co.uk/glassman)

Features:

* Overview of key methods of psychological research
* Student friendly pedagogy including discussion points and queries, clear chapter summaries, key terms and concepts defined in context
* Annotated suggestions for further reading
* Extensive glossary and bibliography

This clear and concise exploration of psychology is key reading for students new to the discipline.

Contents

512pp   0 335 21348 0

www.openup.co.uk/glassman

Open up your options

Education

Health & Social Welfare

Management

Media, Film & Culture

Psychology & Counselling

Sociology

Study Skills

for more information on our
publications visit **www.openup.co.uk**

OPEN UNIVERSITY PRESS
McGraw - Hill Education